BOOZE-INFUSED DINNERS
IN 40 MINUTES OR LESS

THE SMASHED CHEF PRESENTS:

BOOZE-INFUSED DINNERS IN 40 MINUTES OR LESS

THE JOY OF "SPIRITED" COOKING

BY THE SMASHED CHEF

CONTENTS

ABOUT THE SMASHED CHEF

The Smashed Chef was born in 1969, in Marseilles France to American parents infected by wanderlust. (Yes, I sometimes speak in the 3rd person.)

Like a seed hitched to the pant leg of my parents, who seemed to read their passports more than they read to me as a youth, I was a world traveler from the tender age of 9 months. By the time I was 2, my father had served me my first goblet of diluted wine. (Because that's what they do in France of course…)

I lived in Europe enjoying the culture and food until my early teens. Then India, Turkey, finally moving to Singapore and then Bangkok. My culinary viewpoint has been forged by many countries and many cultures.

As a result of my frequent travels, I have experienced the foods of many nations. Through my mother's passion for cooking, (she started teaching me at 7 years old), I discovered a love for exotic spices and lost cooking techniques. And my globetrotting gave me a unique opportunity to pick and choose the aspects I enjoyed the most.

I attended a top-flight culinary school back in Europe when I reached adulthood. Regrettably, I was kicked out because of my rebellious nature and love of drink.

It took me a few years to "get my life together." After I sobered up from the partying lifestyle of restaurant work, I graduated from a small (but elite) culinary program in America.

Immediately, I used my intimate knowledge of rare spices and little-known techniques to become a private chef for high profile corporate CEO's and finicky rock stars in America, and around the world.

My unique style of infusing alcoholic beverages into each of my dishes has made me sought after by the privileged. I still enjoy beer, wine and spirits, but now in moderation. And my greatest gift to you is putting the *fun* back into cooking.

My unique dishes are simple, speedy and sumptuous... and most of all FUN to prepare.

Now, enjoy a sip or 2 of your favorite libation and create these inspiring, fresh, exquisitely gourmet dishes made in 40 minutes or less.

DEDICATION

Of all of the amazing women on Earth, I am grateful you are in my life. You fill me with love, passion and I promise to never take you for granted My Sweet. It's still magic when you walk into the room. Birds sing, bells ring and people feel warmed as if they were kissed by the sun. Your love of my cuisine has inspired me to share with the rest of the goddesses (and gods) of the world.

To you, my busy reader. Savor these dishes with those you love. Fill yourself with spirits (Responsibly). Bathe your family and your friends in aroma. And do it quickly. My dishes will make you a luminary. I give you the gift of sumptuous gourmet dishes in 40 minutes or less. (Plus a few that take a bit longer for those days you want to feel the joy of food artistry).

Most of all I hope to put FUN back into your kitchen. You're over-worked as it is.

FREE BONUS: The Smashed Chef's Unique and Intuitive Wine Pairing Guide, Filled with Gourmet Tips & Tricks. *www.lovesharecook.com/smashed-chef.*

PREFACE

Life in America is so fast paced compared to much of the world. You rush to work in the morning, get as much done as you can, then rush home to do more. How do you keep up the pace?

And when do you squeeze in romance?

In Europe, meal time is a welcomed respite from the goings on of the day. The evening meal is lingered over and time slows down. Connections are rekindled over a glass of wine and witty conversation. Living in the moment, all worries and responsibilities get put on the backburner, and unbridled joy and a touch of passion takes its rightful place.

My parents moved to France two months after they honeymooned in Paris. They were both well-educated trust-funders, hopelessly romantic and madly in love. My father took up bicycling and my mother attended every culinary class she could. I was born a year later.

As a small child, I remembered that mealtime was something special. My mother was an accomplished cook by that time. She had a joy for cooking that was contagious. And she added love and romance to every meal.

FREE BONUS: The Smashed Chef's Unique and Intuitive Wine Pairing Guide, Filled with Gourmet Tips & Tricks. *www.lovesharecook.com/smashed-chef.*

Meals were not hastily cooked. After all, mother was blessed with an abundance of time. Wine always flowed and every ingredient was treated with reverence. The evening meal was an occasion every night. It lasted for hours as we lingered over the table, eating slowly and laughing heartily.

When I moved to America, after a lifetime of living abroad as a rolling stone who gathered no moss, I greatly missed that part of European culture. The first several months I lived in Idaho, I had feared mealtime would become mundane the bulk of the time. Of course there were those special moments mixed in, but why wasn't every dining experience exceptional?

It soon dawned on me that it was all up to me to teach all of those around me the joy of incredible food and equally amazing moments we could have each night.

That was the spark that lured in my amazing woman. The meal and the moment. It is a recipe for a miraculous life, void of regret and filled with love and passion.

You deserve such pleasures. I realize you're moving at light speed and you don't have the luxury of hours to cook each evening. That is precisely why I bring you my very first cookbook. Because the less time it takes to create sumptuous booze-infused gourmet fare, the more time you will have for the moments.

My goal is to help you bring more fun into the kitchen. And what could be more fun than cooking with booze? With a glass of wine in hand, you'll giggle your way through each tasty recipe. And you'll delight in knowing you're about to create the moments that make up memories you and your lover and your friends will never forget.

You see, life is a collection of moments. And to live life to its fullest, she with the most moments wins. Creating them with a fine meal each night, whether alone with your lover, with family, or with friends is a gift too rich to refuse.

Food brings us together. And no one is more revered than the cook. You don't have to be a chef to be adored. All you need to do is add the secret ingredient of love.

These booze-infused main dishes will make you a star. They will add life to each dinner conversation and intensify your connections. Yes, food helps create moments.

RECIPES

DRUNKED UP TORTILLA SOUP

COOK TIME: 35 MINUTES

"Did you know Acapulco means, like, 'the place where reeds were destroyed' or something?"

Meeting a new client is always weird. Some of them are super uptight about every little detail. Some of them are incredibly gregarious and try to win me over with the force of their personality. Some are domineering, afraid to cede control of any aspect of their life to an outsider. Some are just plain crazy.

Still, it took me aback when my new client opened our first conversation ever with linguistics. I expected something a bit more ballsy from the lead singer of a rock band. Luckily, he didn't disappoint me.

I remember very little of my trip to Acapulco. In between too many tequila shots, I vaguely recall an onslaught of late-night debauchery. Girls in bars, girls on the beach, girls wandering down the street, looking for prey. Oh, and did I mention *too many tequila shots*. I'd call it "over-indulgence," but that still implies some measure of control.

At the end of the night, I head back to my place or (more often than not) somebody else's. Stumble over some misplaced rug. Hopefully make it into bed. Then, wake up at four in the afternoon, drink down the hair of the dog, and do it all over again. With gusto.

Somewhere in this haze, my client and I developed a new ritual. After every night of ritualized sinning, I'd bring him a huge bowl of my "Drunked Up Tortilla Soup", filled with rich corn on the cob and chicken breasts. It helps keep the shots down, and prevents the next-day regret at least a little bit.

Then again, I also served it to him with another shot of tequila.

Ingredients

2 tablespoons peanut oil, plus ¼ to ⅓ cup for drizzling
3 ears corn on the cob, shucked or 2 ears fresh-frozen cobs, defrosted
½ cup dry red wine (Such as Merlot or Cabernet)
1 red bell pepper, halved and seeded
1 pound chicken breast tenders
1 teaspoon poultry seasoning
1 teaspoon cumin
Salt and pepper to taste
1 medium zucchini, diced
1 medium yellow skinned onion, chopped
3 cloves garlic, chopped
1 to 2 chipotle peppers in adobo (medium to hot heat), chopped
1 28-ounce can stewed tomatoes
1 8-ounce can tomato sauce
3 cups chicken stock, pre-packaged works fine
4 cups blue corn tortilla chips, broken into large pieces
1 cup shredded Cheddar or Pepper Jack Cheese
½ cup sour cream
¼ red raw onion, chopped (optional for garnish)
2 to 3 tablespoons chopped cilantro or parsley leaves (optional for garnish)
1 ripe avocado, diced and dressed with the juice of ½ lemon (optional for garnish)
Diced jalapeños (optional for garnish)

Preparation

- Using a griddle pan, drizzle some oil on the corn and place it on griddle. Grill the red pepper along with corn. Char the veggies for ten minutes rotating until done. They should be lightly blackened. Cut off kernels and reserve in a bowl.

- Cool for five minutes and take the skin off the pepper. It should slip off easily. If not, grill it for a minute or two more. (Secret Smashed Chef technique: Put the pepper into a bowl, and put plastic wrap over the top for 5-10 minutes. The heat and humidity will make peeling off the skin a breeze).

- Cube the chicken and add 2 tbsp. oil to your favorite soup pot. You do have a favorite, don't you? If not, go shopping for one.

- Add the chicken and seasonings, including cumin, salt, pepper and poultry seasoning. Add your wine and veggies, allowing the veggies to soften over 5-7 minutes.

4

- Add the tomatoes, stock, and tomato paste last. Then, let the mixture boil. Turn to low, and put your lovely grilled corn into the soup. Chop red pepper and add to soup. Fold in chips and serve soup with shredded cheese, avocado, jalapeno and sour cream as desired for garnishes.
- Consume with gusto, like a rock star. You just may think you're enjoying a vacation to the warm climes of the Mexican Riviera...

Smashed Chef Secrets: *A microwave can save you a lot of time shucking corn. Cut off ear about one inch above the last row of kernels and microwave for two to three minutes. Hold the uncut end, shake and squeeze the husk until the corn slides out. Easy peasy!*

FREE BONUS: The Smashed Chef's Unique and Intuitive Wine Pairing Guide, Filled with Gourmet Tips & Tricks. *www.lovesharecook.com/smashed-chef.*

5

SURF AND TURF POTATO SOUP

COOK TIME: 40 MINUTES

It's Cape Cod, Massachusetts, and I'm with a group of friends in a store that sells inflatable rafts and stuff for the ocean. We're doing what we do best, a.k.a. being drunk and disorderly. Our favorite game is pointing out the most ridiculous pool toys to each other. It's in the course of this game that I see Marty.

Marty, my dear reader, is an octopus. A giant, six-foot-tall, inflatable octopus. From the moment our eyes lock, it's love at first drunken sight. I know I've got to save Marty. I gather my friends and I tell them what we have to do. We have to rescue this poor octopus from the confines of captivity.

Our sober friend, "Jim," tries to object. "What the 'H-E-Double Hockey Sticks' are we going to do with an inflatable octopus?" he asks. He is summarily overruled, and watches helplessly as we acquire Marty from the annoyed shop owner and tie the newly-freed octopus to the roof. We, then, command Jim to drive to the beach.

Once there, we all set to building a fire on the sand. We set Marty up next to the fire pit with a marshmallow roaster and a cold beer while we watch the sun go down. Marty turns out to be a great wingman. Girls flock to our little group to sit on Marty's lap and drink beers with us. As the sun falls below the horizon, however, I nod to my friends and then to Marty. "It's been great knowing you Marty! I hope you've enjoyed your first day of freedom as much as we've enjoyed showing you this beautiful world. Now go out there and make something of yourself!"

We pushed Marty out to sea, past the breakers, and then we left him swimming out there in his natural habitat. We never heard from Marty again. Afterward, we went home and I made a huge pot of this ocean-inspired soup to honor our dear departed friend Marty, the inflatable octopus from Cape Cod.

6

Ingredients

½ stick butter
1 small onion, diced
1 pound medium shrimp
4½ cups milk, whole, reduced fat (2 percent) or low fat (1 percent)
¼ cup white wine (Chardonnay would work)
2 medium carrots, diced
2 tablespoons all-purpose flour
8 medium russet potatoes, peeled and cubed
2 chicken bouillon cubes
1 cup half and half
1 teaspoon Celtic sea salt
¼ teaspoon pepper
2 cups lightly salted water
Crumbled bacon bits, for garnish
Grated sharp Cheddar Cheese, for garnish
Dill sprigs or parsley, for garnish (optional)

Preparation

- Heat ½ cup of milk, drop in the bouillon cubes, and allow them to dissolve.

- Using a large, deep pan, allow the butter to melt, and then sauté the onion in the white wine.

- While you see that wine bottle, pour yourself a glass. You already did? Well played.

- Add the carrots, and let them soften for about five minutes. Whisk the flour into the mixture, and add the remaining milk, bouillon (already dissolved together), and, of course, the potatoes. Cook on medium for fifteen minutes or until potatoes get soft. Mix in the half and half. Salt and pepper to taste.

- Then, in a smaller pan, bring to boil the salted water and add shrimp to cook, about 2-3 minutes. Don't let those shrimp linger in the pan. Overcooked shrimp is criminal. Drain shrimp, peel, devein, and chop until chunky. Add shrimp to soup base, and serve with grated cheese and bacon bits on top if you like. Or perhaps a sprig of parsley, if you're trying to score points with your lover.

- Devour with crusty bread and a salad. Say hi to Marty if you see him.

FREE BONUS: The Smashed Chef's Unique and Intuitive Wine Pairing Guide, Filled with Gourmet Tips & Tricks. *www.lovesharecook.com/smashed-chef.*

7

SPICY BLACK BEAN SOUP

COOK TIME: 35 MINUTES

Ah, San Antonio. Land of the Alamo. It was there that I came up with this spicy, TexMex-inspired soup, chock full of bacon and black beans.

It was also where I talked to a donkey.

And I swear he talked back!

I don't know how much I drank that night, but it was more than enough to put me a little over the edge. As my friends shepherded me home, I looked across the street and saw a donkey standing on the sidewalk.

Now, from here on out my memory is a bit hazy. According to my friends, I sprinted across the street like a madman. I then recall talking to the donkey, asking him where he worked and what type of food he liked. I also asked him whether he'd like to come home with us, and was furious when my friends started dragging me away without bringing our donkey friend along.

Especially since I think my new donkey pal just said he wanted a bottle of Mescal and I could have the worm...

When I awoke the next day, my friends of course took great pleasure at informing me the donkey was part of a logo for a local restaurant, and I had been talking to a painted wall the whole time.

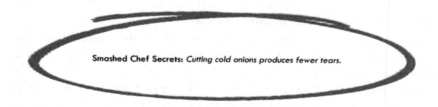

Smashed Chef Secrets: *Cutting cold onions produces fewer tears.*

Ingredients

10 slices bacon, finely chopped
2 medium onions, chopped (about 2 ½ cups)
6 garlic cloves, pressed
$^1/_3$ cup whiskey
1 14½-ounce can reduced-sodium chicken broth
1½ cups canned chopped tomatoes
2 tablespoons ketchup
2 teaspoons Worcestershire sauce
1 tablespoon chili powder
4 15½-ounce cans black beans, drained but not rinsed
Kosher salt and freshly ground black pepper to taste
1 bunch fresh cilantro
Juice of ½ lime
Thinly sliced scallions, for garnish
Sour cream, for garnish
Grated Cheddar Cheese, for garnish

Preparation

- Cook the bacon for about 4 minutes, then add the onions, cooking another four minutes.
- Stir in whiskey. Add the garlic and cook an additional minute. Add the tomatoes, broth, ketchup, chili powder, and Worcestershire sauce. Finally, stir the beans into the mixture and turn pan on high so that it boils. Simmer at a gentle boil for ten minutes, uncovered. Salt and pepper to taste.
- Take cilantro and discard the thick stems. Chop, then stir into soup. The soup should be thick by now. Add the lime juice in at the last minute.
- Put this delicious concoction in bowls and top with garnishes as noted above.

FREE BONUS: The Smashed Chef's Unique and Intuitive Wine Pairing Guide, Filled with Gourmet Tips & Tricks. *www.lovesharecook.com/smashed-chef.*

9

ORGASMIC THAI POTATO CURRY

COOK TIME: 25 MINUTES

She's cute. At least, I hope it's a she. This is Thailand, after all, and they're known as much for their ladyboy industry as they are for their delicious curries...

After downing the rest of my Thai Rice whisky, (the Smashed Chef never wastes a drop, and neither should *you*), I go over and introduce myself. At first she's not having any of it, but I'm nothing if not persistent. Still, nothing seems to be working until I mention I'm a chef.

I'd be lying if I said her response was encouraging: "Bull manure" is, I think, the appropriate term.

Now, I've got her though. She's intrigued, if nothing else, and—more importantly—she's wrong. I may be a womanizing boozer by night, but hand me a good knife, fresh ingredients, and a few pans...

I take her back to my place, and immediately start preparing my best Thai curry. It's quick and easy, but it *looks* and *tastes* impressive. Living in Bangkok, I'd learned the secret to a great Thai curry—replace the stock with a light Thai lager instead. In goes half a cup of Singha, a light lager, and twenty minutes later we're ready to eat.

One bite, and her eyes grew wide with wonder. Two bites, she was ready to eat out of my hand. Three bites, her eyes rolled back in her head, and I'd swear she was on the verge of an orgasm. We're talking moans, gasps, and all.

What kind of villain would I be if I just left her like that, hot and bothered? It didn't take long for us to forget the curry, though it also made for good leftovers the next day.

Ingredients

2 teaspoons peanut oil
1 large onion chopped
2½ teaspoons Thai Green Curry Paste (prepared, in the Asian aisle of the grocery store)
1 pound red-skin potatoes, skin on, cut into ½ inch cubes,
⅓ cup coconut milk
½ cup lager beer
1 14½ ounce can canned crushed tomatoes
1 tablespoon fresh squeezed lime juice
1 tablespoon fresh basil, chopped
Dash of red pepper flakes
3 cups cooked rice, hot

Preparation

- In a large wok or big skillet, heat oil over medium-high heat. Add the onion and stir-fry it until golden, about 5 minutes. Add curry paste and stir in for 1 minute. It will get quite fragrant over your wok. Brace yourself. Have a sip of wine after you're done.
- Nice. Let's move on...
- Add the potatoes and toss well to evenly coat them in the curry. Add the coconut milk and your lager. Add the can of crushed tomatoes along with the juice to wok. Cover and simmer until potatoes are tender and done, about 15 to 20 minutes. Then, stir in lime juice and add chopped basil. Serve over rice. Garnish with crushed red pepper flakes.
- Enjoy a nice dinner with the escort of your choice, transgender or not.

FREE BONUS: The Smashed Chef's Unique and Intuitive Wine Pairing Guide, Filled with Gourmet Tips & Tricks. *www.lovesharecook.com/smashed-chef.*

ll

SPEEDY SMASHED AND SPICY TOMATO SOUP

COOK TIME: 25 MINUTES

Sometimes, I get lucky.

Despite what conclusion your brain may have leapt towards, I'm actually talking about cooking. I strongly believe that desperation is a key ingredient to genius. On a sunny day in Tuscany, I was *desperate* to get out of the house and hit the town with a lovely lady at my side. I had a full night of decadence planned.

First, I had to take care of that pesky "eating" problem, however. In the best Smashed Chef fashion, I grabbed a bunch of ingredients I had lying around and tossed them into a big pot. Marinara sauce, chicken, cannellini beans, carrots, and some pasta for texture and added flavor—all thrown on the stove.

At first I thought it might be the copious amounts of wine clouding my judgment, but when I revisited the recipe a week later I knew I had a real winner. This variation of classic tomato soup is spicy, hearty, and healthy while taking almost no time to prepare, leaving you with plenty of time for "other" activities.

Ingredients

3 tablespoons olive oil
2 carrots, peeled and chopped
1 small onion, chopped
1 clove garlic, minced
¼ cup gin
1 26-ounce jar good marinara sauce
2 14-ounce cans chicken broth
1 15-ounce can cannellini beans, drained and rinsed
½ teaspoon red pepper flakes
½ cup pastina pasta (or any small pasta)
½ teaspoon salt
½ teaspoon freshly ground black pepper

Preparation

This is going to be fast. Pour yourself a Gin and Tonic if you like. FYI: this soup is best made while desperate, for maximum flavor.

- Heat the olive oil in your soup pot and add veggies, sautéing over medium heat for about 2 minutes or until soft.
- Add the gin and stir it in. Add the marinara sauce along with cannellini beans, chicken broth, pasta, red pepper flakes, and salt and pepper to taste. Let this simmer uncovered for ten minutes before serving.
- Just enough time to finish that Gin and Tonic. Pour another.

WHISKEY CHICKEN CHORIZO STEW

COOK TIME: 35 MINUTES

My mother always claimed that she kept whiskey on-hand for cooking recipes like this one, but I'm sure it didn't help that I was a terror to deal with.

Nevertheless, twenty-three years later and halfway around the world, this recipe came back to me. I was living the life. One of my clients, a singer/songwriter I'll refer to from here on out as "Tom," had flown me to his private Mexican villa to cook for him and some friends.

Now, if ever there were a building more deserving of the name "Whiskey a Go-Go" than the club in Hollywood, it was this villa. Why, you ask? Tom had more whiskey on hand than I've ever seen before or since. He had whiskey of all types, from all around the world. Many nights passed by in a Makers Mark induced blur of gorgeous women and loud music.

One day, browsing through the brightly-colored marketplace for a new hangover cure, I saw a package of chorizo and my mom's old recipe came racing back.

"Could you be any damn louder?" Tom said as he walked into my kitchen. He stopped short. "What am I smelling?" His eyes grew wide.

"Makers Mark, chorizo, garlic, tomatoes, some chicken..." I said, handing him a full bowl and a couple of tortillas on the side.

Needless to say, the party continued that night. And still I have no idea if I scored...

Ingredients

1 pound chicken tenders
Salt and pepper to taste
1/3 cup whiskey
3/4 pound chorizo sausage, diced (in the packaged meats case near Kielbasa)
2 tablespoons extra-virgin olive oil
3 cloves garlic, smashed
1 red bell pepper, seeded and chopped
1 medium onion, chopped
6 small red potatoes, diced
1 15-ounce can fire roasted chopped tomatoes
1 15-ounce can dark red kidney beans, drained
2 teaspoons hot sauce
1 quart chicken stock
1 sack red or blue corn tortilla chips
2 cups shredded Pepper Jack or Smoked Cheddar Cheese
Suggested garnishes: chopped scallions, chopped cilantro or fresh thyme leaves

Preparation

Have you found a favorite soup pot yet? Now is the time to use it. Perhaps you should break it in with whiskey... Smashed Chef style.

- Let your soup pot get hot over medium heat. Chop the chicken, but not too loudly. Don't encourage your hangover. Season with salt and pepper.

- Once the pot is heated, cook the chicken with olive oil for 2 minutes and add chorizo, garlic and whiskey (be careful of the vapors if you have a gas stove). Cook for an additional 2-3 minutes.

- Add potatoes, onions, and peppers, then cook for another 5 minutes. Finally, put in the tomatoes, beans, and hot sauce. Add the chicken stock, and let your heavenly hangover cure reach a slow boil. It should be nice and soupy now. Let the stew simmer, uncovered, for ten minutes to make the potatoes soft and luxurious.

- Now preheat the broiler. Fill individual soup bowls two-thirds full with the crushed tortilla chips. Top with the cheese. Melt the cheese under the broiler. Use scallions and herbs to garnish the soup.

- Take a bite, and duel that hangover to the death.

FREE BONUS: The Smashed Chef's Unique and Intuitive Wine Pairing Guide, Filled with Gourmet Tips & Tricks. *www.lovesharecook.com/smashed-chef.*

15

ITALIAN WHITE BEAN VINO SOUP

COOK TIME: 20 MINUTES

"Closed? Closed! CLOSED?!"

Apologies, reader, but I'm afraid I threw a bit of a tantrum when I saw that my favorite Brooklyn diner had shut down. Apologies to the wall that I punched, also. The restaurant wasn't a place you'd know, probably. It was a no-name joint on a no-name street in a quiet part of town.

I can't say how good their food was in general, because I only ever ate one thing there: the Italian White Bean Vino Soup. I'd like to say that I took the news of this diner's demise with some measure of poise, but I'd be lying. Instead, I went into mourning.

What do I, the Smashed Chef, do when I mourn? Well, I think the colloquial phrasing would be, "I drink too much." I do not recommend this method of mourning to anyone, but my younger self didn't know better. I went home, drew the curtains, threw on some sad tunes from yesteryear, and poured a drink. And another.

It was later that night, halfway through the next bottle of white wine, that I had a realization. "Wait a minute—I'm a damned *chef.*"

To the kitchen I went, though with all the swaying it seemed to resemble a ship's galley more than anything else. I pulled out all the ingredients I could remember and cooked my own version of that glorious soup. Deliciously light, rich in flavor and texture, this meal feels thick even as it keeps you thin. Make sure to mash half the beans in the soup to get an authentic Tuscan texture!

Ingredients

2 tablespoons butter
1 tablespoon olive oil
2 shallots, chopped
½ cup dry white wine
1 sage leaf
2 15-ounce cans cannellini beans
    drained and rinsed
4 cups low-sodium chicken broth
4 cloves garlic, cut in ½
½ cup cream
½ teaspoon freshly ground black pepper
6 slices Ciabatta bread
Extra-virgin olive oil, for drizzling

Preparation

Channel your inner Italian alcoholic tonight. Pour a glass of Pinot Grigio. Let's cook!

- Preheat your favorite soup pot over medium heat. Put in olive oil, butter, and shallots. Cook about five minutes and add white wine. Your Pinot Grigio is perfect.

- Add the beans and sage to the mixture and then add stock, allowing the mixture to simmer, uncovered. Add garlic until softened, about ten minutes.

- Put the soup in big bowl and puree about half of the soup. Put the blended and unblended soups parts back into the pot. Finally, add cream and pepper to taste. Serve warm with slices of Ciabatta bread that has been drizzled with olive oil and grilled ever so lightly, about three minutes per side. Serve bread with soup.

BABY MEAT-A-BALLA SOUP

COOK TIME: 40 MINUTES

Most people become rebellious in their teenage years. Me? I began my rebellious streak when I decided to stay in the womb an extra week. For proof, look no further than this recipe. When I was only nine, a little old lady tried to teach me how to make meat-a-ballas. Rather than follow her Preparation, I instead made tiny meat-a-ballas. And I was in deep trouble. Again.

If you've never been scolded by an old Italian grandmother, count yourself fortunate. In fact, thank the universe every single day that you haven't been thrown under that bus yet. What happens when an immovable object meets an unstoppable force? Well, if that immovable object is an old Italian grandmother then I can guarantee that unstoppable force will hit you like a ton of bricks. Perhaps like my experience. Perhaps the single greatest tongue-lashing the world has ever heard throughout history and all dimensions of time.

Still, I survived the tongue-lashing and continue to make tiny meat-a-ballas to this day. They're a perfect mouthful of meaty flavor, and definitely help liven up a soup. Be a rebel. Avoid tongue-lashings from old Italian ladies. Eat well and drink heartily.

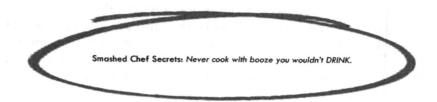

Smashed Chef Secrets: *Never cook with booze you wouldn't DRINK.*

Ingredients

2 tablespoons extra-virgin olive oil
2 carrots, peeled and chopped
2 ribs celery, chopped
1 medium onion, chopped
½ cup dry red wine
2 bay leaves, fresh or dried
Salt and freshly ground black pepper to taste
1 pound ground beef, pork and veal combined
1 egg, beaten
2 cloves garlic, minced
½ cup grated Parmigiano-Reggiano or Romano Cheese
½ cup plain breadcrumbs
½ teaspoon freshly grated or ground nutmeg
6 cups chicken stock or broth
2 cups water
1½ cups dried pasta, rings, broken fettuccini or ditalini
1 pound triple washed fresh spinach, coarsely chopped

Preparation

Pop a bottle of wine. A nice Merlot will do (for the recipe, of course).

- Using a large soup pot on medium heat, add the oil and warm. Now the chopped carrots, onion, celery, and bay leaves go in the pool. Salt and pepper to taste. Add red wine and let veggies cook 5-6 minutes covered. While the vegetables are cooking, savor a sip of the Merlot if you like. You should test it after all.

- Now, mix the meat, egg, grated cheese, garlic, breadcrumbs, nutmeg, salt and pepper. Then, add the broth to the pot and get soup boiling.

- When it boils, lower the heat and make baby meat-a-ballas out of the meat mixture. Put them right in the pot. Then add pasta to the mixture and simmer uncovered for 10 minutes. When the pasta is ready, add chopped spinach until it wilts. Then it is ready to adjust seasonings and serve.

- If you're feeling extra rebellious, flip an old Italian grandmother the bird while you eat this meal. She'll probably send the gesture right back.

QUICK CLAM CHOWDER WITH DEVILED HAM MELTS

COOK TIME: 40 MINUTES

When I was a bit younger, I once met a girl who was part Brazilian, part Japanese. While at first it seemed like a strange pairing, I soon found out what a blessing it was. She perfectly embodied raw sexual prowess and stamina, but tempered this ferocity with litheness and grace. It was a match made in heaven (or, seeing how sinful she was, hell).

This clam chowder is much like that beautiful woman. Is it New England style chowder? Manhattan style? How about both? The potatoes give it a rich, New England-style texture, but the hot sauce adds a dash of Manhattan. Plus, it's got a little Smashed Chef kick to it—wine and bacon finish off the recipe.

Serve it in a mug topped with bread and deviled ham, and you might just find a little bit of Brazil and Japan in your lover tonight. Not a bad return on your investment, for forty minutes of work.

Ingredients

2 tablespoons butter
2 slices thick cut bacon, chopped
1 medium onion, chopped
½ cup dry white wine
2 ribs celery with greens, chopped
4 sprigs fresh thyme
Salt and pepper to taste
2 teaspoons hot sauce
2 tablespoons all-purpose flour
1 pint half and half
2 cups chicken stock
1 cup hash brown style raw shredded potatoes, from dairy aisle of the market
2 6½ ounce cans whole baby clams and their juice
Deviled Ham Melts:
2 sandwich size English muffins, split
¾ pound boiled deli ham, chopped
1 tablespoon paprika

2 tablespoons hot sauce
3 to 4 tablespoons yellow mustard, squirt top bottle – eyeball it
A handful parsley, curly or flat
8 deli slices, about 8 to 10 ounces, white Sharp Cheddar

Preparation

Yes, there is a bit going on with this dish, but it really goes fast. And, in the end, it's what you always really dreamed clam chowder would taste like.

- Take a medium pan and put on medium heat long enough to melt butter. Let it melt. Add the onions, celery, bacon and white wine. Throw thyme sprigs into the pool. Add seasonings of salt, pepper, and hot sauce. Allow the whole mixture to cook for 5 minutes.
- (Just enough time for a glass or two of wine.)
- Stir in the flour and cook for an additional minute. You are making a roux! How awesome is that? Then put in half and half and the stock. Allow to boil, then add in clams and potatoes.
- Gently boil soup for a minute before allowing it to simmer for fifteen minutes. Your soup should be thick and clamilicious.
- Now, turn on your broiler and toast the split English muffins. Grind up the ham along with the paprika, mustard, hot sauce, and parsley using a food processor. Put the ham mixture on top of the muffins and put two slices of cheese on top. Melt the cheese under your broiler.
- Take thyme sprigs out of soup. Get your seasonings right. (Smashed Chef Secret: Always taste EVERY DISH before serving, adjust seasoning if needed. That will give your diners the BEST first impression of your cooking prowess.) Now put the soup in mugs with muffins on top.
- Put it on the table along with another bottle of Chardonnay. Tell your lover your relationship is missing a bit of Brazil and Japan. Get slapped. Actually, don't tell your lover that at all.

FREE BONUS: The Smashed Chef's Unique and Intuitive Wine Pairing Guide, Filled with Gourmet Tips & Tricks. *www.lovesharecook.com/smashed-chef.*

21

HOOCHED UP CREAMY BROCCOLI SOUP
WITH CROUTONS

COOK TIME: 40 MINUTES

What kind of trouble could you possibly get up to at a farm? Nothing, right? Especially a farm that specializes in *broccoli*—sounds like the antithesis of my normal Smashed Chef habitat.

Soon after arriving at said broccoli farm, however, I found out that my circumstances weren't quite as dire as they seemed. My host, an actor and sometimes brewer, greeted me with a big smile and a Mason jar of good ol' country moonshine. Have you ever had a drink that felt like your chest was going to light on fire? Multiply that by three and you've got your standard country moonshine.

"To one hell of a night," I said to my host and his friends, raising my glass jar.

Of course, a bunch of crazed drunks in the middle of the countryside couldn't stop with just lighting their insides on fire. We had to set a bonfire too. Ten minutes in, the wood started to snap, crackle, and pop. Twenty minutes in, the fire was roaring like a crazed lion. An hour in, we were running out of wood at a prodigious rate. That was when my host, drunker even than yours truly, started pulling furniture from his house and burning that too. Into the fire went an old wooden futon, a broken side-table, a chair.

Just a normal night in the countryside, according to my host. And *that*, my friends, is the story of how I swore off moonshine.

Luckily, staring into the flaming remains of my host's living room furniture, I came up with this recipe. Whiskey only—no need to make your own hooch. Add broccoli, heavy cream, and homemade croutons and you've got a great country recipe that tastes good at any time of year.

Seriously, though, be careful around that moonshine. It packs a mean wallop.

Ingredients

4 tablespoons butter, room temperature
1½ pounds fresh broccoli
1 large onion, chopped
¼ cup whiskey
1 carrot, chopped
Salt and freshly ground black pepper to taste
3 tablespoons all-purpose flour
4 cups low-sodium chicken broth
½ cup cream
Homemade Croutons, recipe follows

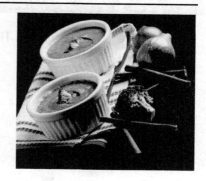

Preparation

Unless you're cooking for George HW Bush, everyone will like this soup. The whiskey will sell them, trust me on that.

- Put the butter in medium pan and melt it. It will soften quickly from the heat. Add the onions, carrots, broccoli, salt, and pepper. Sauté until onions are clear—approximately 6 minutes.

- Add whiskey and flour and cook for a minute until flour turns slightly yellow. Add stock and gently boil the mixture. Then turn to simmer and cook uncovered for 15 minutes.

- Put in the cream and mix. Take an immersion blender and puree the entirety of the soup. Or puree it in a Vitamix if you have one. That makes it super easy. Salt and pepper to taste.

- Serve with homemade croutons made with day old French bread, salt, pepper, olive oil, and a quarter teaspoon of red pepper flakes. Take these ingredients and mix together. Set oven to 400 degrees and spread onto baking sheet. Cook in oven for 15 minutes and serve in soup.

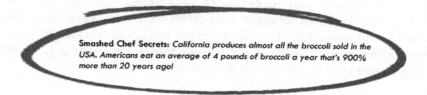

Smashed Chef Secrets: *California produces almost all the broccoli sold in the USA. Americans eat an average of 4 pounds of broccoli a year that's 900% more than 20 years ago!*

GIN JOINT ITALIAN VEGGIE SOUP

COOK TIME: 35 MINUTES

"Ah, the martini.
Such a classy drink."

That's what I always tell myself, after I've already had far too many drinks for the night. Maybe it's the chef in me, but I always feel like I can trick myself into drinking more as long as it's a "worthy" drink with good ingredients. A classic drink. The kind of drink that never goes out of style.

I'd say the martini is actually my worst enemy, because I tend to only drink them when I'm rounding out the night and don't actually need more liquor in my system. But, hey, I'm holding a classy drink even as I sway back and forth, and that's all that matters. Appearances are everything my dear reader.

The gin in this vegetable-based soup will add a little zest to the mix and help convince you to eat more vegetables. Vegetables are important for their antioxidant properties, and will keep you slim, healthy, and beautiful. Still, they're often neglected in favor of other, less-healthy options. Why don't all vegetables taste just a bit more like alcohol? I'd certainly eat more of them.

Ingredients

1 (15-ounce) can low-sodium cannellini beans, drained and rinsed
1 tablespoon olive oil
½ large onion, diced
2 carrots, diced
2 stalks celery, diced,
1 small zucchini, diced
1 clove garlic, minced
1 tablespoon chopped fresh thyme leaves (or 1 teaspoon dried)
2 teaspoons chopped fresh sage leaves (or ½ teaspoon dried)
½ teaspoon salt
¼ teaspoon freshly ground black pepper
¼ cup gin
32 ounces low-sodium chicken broth or vegetable broth
1 14½ -ounce can no salt added diced tomatoes
2 cups chopped baby spinach leaves
⅓ cup freshly grated Parmesan, optional

Preparation

- Take a masher and smash half the beans. Set this half of the beans aside.

- In a large soup pot add oil, onions, celery, zucchini, carrots, garlic, sage, thyme, salt and pepper, and heat on medium high. When the vegetables are tender, add the gin, broth, and tomatoes. And let the mixture gently boil. Add the whole beans and the smashed beans. Add spinach until it wilts, about 3 minutes or so. Serve with grated Parmesan cheese on top.

- Now you've made vegetables taste like alcohol. I knew you were a hero. World class. Go drink a martini while you're at it.

FREE BONUS: The Smashed Chef's Unique and Intuitive Wine Pairing Guide, Filled with Gourmet Tips & Tricks. *www.lovesharecook.com/smashed-chef.*

25

ARTICHOKE SOUP A LA VINO

COOK TIME: 40 MINUTES

Ah, Sonoma County. One of the last havens for rich assholes with too much time and money on their hands. My kind of clients! Lucky for me, I've been known to be an asshole from time to time, even if I'm not exactly using hundred dollar bills as toilet paper yet.

Let's get this straight: Napa is pretty much heaven for the Smashed Chef. It practically rains wine. Beautiful women grow up like dewy, fresh sprouts from the ground. Thus, I rejoiced when I found myself in Napa with a group of ill-reputed friends.

Napa, of course, did not rejoice. Nay, if ever there were a time when locusts descended on the fruitful valley, it was when my friends and I arrived in this glorious land of grapes. By the time night fell on our first day, we were all utterly sloshed, having made a day of draining California's most delicious wine offerings. Of course you can under-stand my confusion when I awoke in a strange kitchen in a strange house with none of my friends around. Oh, and also, a pot of soup simmering on the stove. Oh, and a woman screaming that there was some drunken, dirty hobo in their house. Naturally, I yelled back that I was on a Joseph Phelps Vineyard bender and while perhaps I smell like a mule – I am NOT a hobo!

Yes, friends, don't black out and cook. *Especially* not in a random bed and breakfast in Napa. Lucky for me, the owners knew that ne'er-do-wells don't go to a vineyard as fine as Joseph Phelps. Plus, they enjoyed my artichoke soup enough that they decided not to press any charges. Instead they offered me a shower, we ate a great lunch, and then they sent me on my way with Preparation back to my hotel. Oh, and they gave me a case of their finest Chardonnay in return for the recipe. I'm the Smashed Chef; I couldn't say no to that kind of deal.

Ingredients

2 tablespoons extra-virgin olive oil
2 leeks, white part only, washed well and chopped
1 clove garlic, minced
½ cup white wine
1 small potato, peeled and chopped
1 8-ounce package frozen artichoke hearts, thawed
2 cups chicken stock
½ teaspoon salt
¼ teaspoon freshly ground black pepper
2 tablespoons plus ⅓ cup mascarpone cheese
2 tablespoons chopped chives, for garnish

Preparation

■ Using a large soup pot over medium heat, allow the olive oil to heat up. Add the garlic and the leeks and stir. Add the potatoes and cook for five minutes. Add artichokes, white wine, stock and spices. Allow to cook 20 minutes or until veggies are soft.

■ Now go to your computer and find out more about taking a trip to wine country. You deserve it.

■ Now back to your soup.

■ Puree the soup in batches with a blender or with a handheld immersion blender. Add 2 tbsp. mascarpone, blending further and reserve the ⅓ cup of it to soften for a topping. Put the soup into serving bowls and top each with a spoonful of mascarpone cheese to garnish. Sprinkle with chives.

■ Serve with your favorite white wine. Just make sure it's your kitchen you're cooking in tomorrow.

LOOPY LEMONY CHICKEN SOUP

COOK TIME: 40 MINUTES

It may surprise you to find out that I've been known to get a bit...belligerent when drunk. Sometimes the verbal abuse I spout at unwitting victims is wholly undeserved. Other times, verbal abuse is the least I can do.

Such was the case on one occasion while I was visiting Italy. I was sitting at a restaurant with my friend, "Mark," when he said he was tired of eating real Parmesan cheese. No, he wanted to shake out his own from a silly green can.

A CAN!

Them's fightin' words. Whether it was the hot Italian sun that set me off or the bottle of heavy Sangiovese I'd consumed already, I don't know. But I was determined not to let Mark's slight go. By all accounts, I'm lucky he still considers me a friend. My only clear memory is calling him a "Cheese Philistine" while gesticulating around the restaurant. And then being asked to leave by the manager.

I stomped out of the restaurant in a rage, my food only half-eaten. On the way home I picked up some real Parmesan cheese, rind and all, from a fine artisanal cheese maker. By combining the salty, flavorful rind with some rich white wine, roasted chicken, lemon juice, and a bay leaf (amongst other ingredients) I created the following recipe. Hey, even Mark admitted he was wrong after just one bite.

Ingredients

6 cups low-sodium chicken broth
⅓ cup fresh lemon juice (about 2 lemons)
½ cup dry white wine
1 dried bay leaf
1 2-inch piece Parmesan cheese rind, optional
2 medium carrots, peeled and sliced into ¼-inch pieces
1 cup (about 2½ ounces) spaghetti, broken into 2-inch pieces
2 cups diced cooked rotisserie chicken, preferably breast meat
1 cup grated Romano cheese
¼ cup chopped fresh flat-leaf parsley
Kosher salt and freshly ground pepper to taste

Preparation

A dry white wine goes well with this dish. Do uncork a bottle right now and let it breathe. Now pour a glass, drink it down, and let's get cooking.

- In a big pot, put in the chicken broth, lemon juice, white wine, bay leaf and parmesan rind. Boil this on high. That releases the magic of your parmesan rind. Screw you, Mark.

- Add carrots and cook on medium low about 5-8 minutes or until carrots are soft. Add broken pieces of pasta and cook for up to 5 minutes or until al dente. Add chicken and cook an additional 2-3 minutes.

- Scoop out the bay leaf and parmesan rind. Put in half of the cheese and the parsley. Add salt and pepper to taste. Put soup in bowls and top each with a spoonful of the remaining cheese.

- Prepare for deliciousness. This soup goes well with crusty bread. And friends who appreciate good Parmesan.

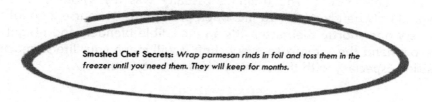

Smashed Chef Secrets: *Wrap parmesan rinds in foil and toss them in the freezer until you need them. They will keep for months.*

FREE BONUS: The Smashed Chef's Unique and Intuitive Wine Pairing Guide, Filled with Gourmet Tips & Tricks. *www.lovesharecook.com/smashed-chef.*

DRUNKEN CAULIFLOWER SOUP
WITH TOASTY DIPPERS

COOK TIME: 35 MINUTES

The Vitamix should be crowned King of the Blenders. It's durable, it's reliable, and it chops things I never knew could be chopped before. It's something every chef should own. That's why the day I finally got one I was determined to throw a party.

As the Smashed Chef, I figured the best way to celebrate a new blender was with mixed drinks. Before long, it was margarita time at the Smashed Chef's secret lair, and the party was heating up. It was around my sixth or seventh margarita that I had one of my greatest worst ideas. An idea that would change the course of the entire night and end in tragedy.

If you've ever seen the popular YouTube series "Will it Blend?", I'm sure you know what comes next. Drunk enough to not recognize trivial things like consequences, I thought it would be a great idea to start throwing random items from around my house into the Vitamix. Just to see what would happen. Though, I take most of the responsibility for my actions, I must say that it isn't like anyone tried to stop me. In fact, I distinctly remember most people shamelessly urging me on.

Results of that night:

Sunglasses? Blended. Deodorant? Blended. Keys? Did not blend. iPhone? Blended. Wallet? Did not blend.

I don't know how many things we broke, but—judging by the large pile of debris next to the blender on the following morn—it was a substantial amount. The ultimate casualty was my Vitamix, which would only barely stutter to life when prompted. Of course, I bought a new one shortly thereafter. It's an incredible blender, and I highly recommend the Vitamix to every chef; it will make your life so much easier. Especially with this whiskey-infused, spicy soup.

Ingredients

1 tablespoon extra virgin olive oil
3 tablespoons butter
Coarse salt and coarsely ground black pepper
½ cup whiskey
2 small heads cauliflower, or 1 large, cut into small bunches of florets
3 ribs celery and leafy tops from the heart of stalk, finely chopped
1 medium onion, chopped
2 tablespoons chopped fresh thyme leaves
2 tablespoons all-purpose flour
1 quart chicken broth
1 cup half and half or whole milk
Hot sauce to taste (optional)
3 tablespoons fresh parsley leaves or chives, chopped for garnish
½ cup grated Parmesan, for passing at the table

Dippers

3 sandwich-size sourdough English muffins, split
3 tablespoons butter
1 garlic clove, minced
Grated Cheddar and Parmesan cheese
Paprika

Preparation

- Take a big pot and heat olive oil and 2 tablespoons of butter on medium heat. Season the pot with salt and pepper and add cauliflower florets. Put in thyme, onion, celery, and whiskey, and cook it for 3 minutes (remember to be careful with the vapors if you have a small pot and cook with gas).

- Move the veggies to one side of the pot, and melt the remaining tablespoon of butter on the empty part of your pan. Mix the flour with butter, cooking for a minute, while stirring the mixture continuously.

- Add the half and half and chicken broth. Stir all the ingredients together and simmer, uncovered, mixture for 15 minutes. Take an immersion blender and puree the soup until smooth (or use a Vitamix if you have one).

FREE BONUS: The Smashed Chef's Unique and Intuitive Wine Pairing Guide, Filled with Gourmet Tips & Tricks. *www.lovesharecook.com/smashed-chef.*

31

- Put the soup back in the pot. Season with hot sauce and other seasonings. Pour into bowls and use hot pepper sauce to garnish along with parsley, chives, or grated cheese (or all three!).
- For the dippers, preheat your broiler and toast the halves of the English muffin. Melt butter and cook garlic over low heat in small skillet. Brush the garlic butter on the muffins and add grated Parmesan and cheddar cheese. Put paprika over cheeses and melt under your broiler. Cut English muffin pieces into rectangular pieces for dipping into soup.
- Check the location of your sunglasses and wallet when you're done. Then, hide your Vitamix from your drunken self.

SMASHEY'S WINEY CHEESY SOUP

COOK TIME: 20 MINUTES

In culinary school (the first time around), I was always looking for meals to make on the fly. While my more dedicated classmates were off making gourmet masterpieces, I just wanted to get back to the party. It may sound ironic that I was studying to be a chef while hating to cook for myself, but it was an unfortunate reality. Eating got in the way of more drinking. In fact, it was here that my habit of pouring alcohol into almost every recipe got started.

Still, some great recipes came out of that era. This is one of them. It's easy to make a tasty and rich soup as long as you use plenty of cheese. The added white wine gives it a great kick. Plus, it only takes twenty minutes until it's done. In soup terms, that's nothing at all. Plenty of time for you to get drinking like Hemingway is back in style.

FREE BONUS: The Smashed Chef's Unique and Intuitive Wine Pairing Guide, Filled with Gourmet Tips & Tricks. *www.lovesharecook.com/smashed-chef.*

Ingredients

1 small onion, diced
2 large pimentos, diced
3 tablespoons butter
3 tablespoons all-purpose flour
¼ cup dry white wine
1½ cups chicken stock
1½ cups cream
¾ cup grated Sharp Cheddar Cheese
Salt and black pepper to taste
Dash cayenne pepper, optional
Garnish with a slice of cooked bacon, croutons and sprig of parsley

Preparation

This is a great dish when you're REALLY rushed. Pour yourself a glass of wine.

- Sauté the onion and pimento in butter for 5-7 minutes. Add the flour, white wine, stock, and cream; then cook in the pot until thick, about 10 minutes.
- Finally, add the cheese and stir until the cheese is melted and fully incorporated. Add cayenne pepper, salt, and pepper. Garnish the soup with a slice of bacon, croutons, and sprig of parsley.
- Now, eat, drink, and rush off to drink more afterward. I told you this would be quick.

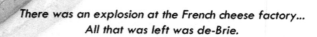

There was an explosion at the French cheese factory...
All that was left was de-Brie.

SAVORY BEAN AND ESCAROLE SOUP

COOK TIME: 22 MINUTES

What are weddings but institutionalized excuses for debauchery? Think about every wedding you've been to. There are always the same scandals. The old man hitting on the young, nubile sister of the groom. The best man and one of the bridesmaids sneaking off together. The distant relative that nobody likes, but who showed up anyway.

And then there's the guy who's always way too drunk. That's me! Not always, and especially not these days, but I've been that guy far too many times in the past. This recipe was actually conceived at one of these ceremonies. I was scheduled to cook at a wedding with 150 guests at my friend's farm-table-restaurant in good ol' Sonoma County (this is the second of three Napa-area tales).

As I tailed a beautiful blonde woman, hoping to strike up a conversation, I stumbled into the most beautiful organic garden. Soon, my eyes lost the lady, and focused on a row of green gold.

I had this soup in mind as I plucked some escarole from that garden (substitute radicchio for escarole if necessary). After a few hours, I had the recipe worked out enough that any little Italian grandmother would've spared me a tongue-lashing, and that's when I unleashed it on the reception.

Of course, I also unleashed myself on the reception. And the ladies. And of course the open bar. Hey, at least the bride liked my recipe enough to ask for a copy. And it's statistically likely that their marriage will end in divorce, so it's not like I ruined their only wedding...

Ingredients

2 tablespoons olive oil
2 garlic cloves, chopped
1 pound escarole, chopped
Salt to taste
4 cups low-salt chicken broth
½ cup dry red wine
1 15-ounce can cannellini beans, drained and rinsed
1 1-ounce piece Parmesan
Freshly ground black pepper
6 teaspoons extra virgin olive oil

Preparation

Prepare to create a masterpiece in a hurry. You've got bridesmaids or groomsmen to hit on. Pre-libate with your favorite wine if you like, especially if you don't know the bride and groom personally.

■ Take 2 tablespoons of olive oil and heat in soup pot on medium. Add the garlic and sauté for about 15 minutes.

■ Put in chopped escarole and sauté until it becomes wilted, about 2 minutes. Add salt. Put in red wine, chicken broth, parmesan cheese and beans. Simmer until completely heated through. It should take only 5 minutes. Add salt and pepper to taste.

SMASHED PUMPKIN BLACk BEAN SOUP

COOK TIME: 22 MINUTES

You know why I love whiskey? It tastes like earth and leather and everything a cowboy needs for a good life. You know why my lovers tend to *not* love whiskey? It tastes like earth and leather and everything a cowboy needs for a good life.

A regrettable paradox.

On the other hand, whiskey seems to make my lovers incredibly frisky. It's a catch-22. I can't convince them to drink it straight, but it's so much fun when they *do* drink it. Thus, I have to sneak it into recipes whenever I can so I get the effects without any of the taste.

That's what happened with this recipe. The whiskey may seem like a weird combination with the pumpkin and black beans, but I guarantee you'll fall in lust with this unique flavor. Just think of the side effects...

Ambiance plays a significant role in creating an aura of romance so make sure your table for two is beautifully decorated.

FREE BONUS: The Smashed Chef's Unique and Intuitive Wine Pairing Guide, Filled with Gourmet Tips & Tricks. *www.lovesharecook.com/smashed-chef.*

37

Ingredients

2 tablespoons extra-virgin olive oil
1 medium onion, finely chopped
¼ cup whiskey
3 cups canned or packaged vegetable stock, found on soup aisle
1 14½-ounce can diced tomatoes in juice
1 15-ounces can black beans, drained
2 15-ounce cans pumpkin puree (found often on the baking aisle)
1 cup heavy cream
1 tablespoon curry powder, 1 palm full
1½ teaspoons ground cumin, ½ palm full
½ teaspoon cayenne pepper,
Coarse salt (I like Celtic sea salt)
20 blades fresh chives, chopped or snipped, for garnish

Preparation

In 22 minutes, you will have brought forth life from this soup. Especially, if you're drunk enough to think the soup is talking to you. Start
drinking.

- Add the oil to a hot soup pot and then add onion, sautéing for 5
  minutes. Add whiskey, broth, black beans, tomatoes, and pumpkin
  (be careful of the whiskey fumes if you use natural gas).

- Stir everything together and bring the soup to the boiling point.
  Set the pot to medium low and put in the spices and cream.
  Simmer for about 5 minutes, then salt and pepper to taste. Garnish
  with chopped up chives.

- Is it talking to you yet? Well then drink more, teetotaler.

38

CHICKEN VINO TORTILLA SOUP

COOK TIME: 35 MINUTES

This recipe also came out of my stint at singer/songwriter client Tom's Mexican villa. In between the constant partying and the nearly constant hangovers, I had a lot of time to come up with new recipes. There's something about the tropical sun, breeze, and unique scents and flavors in Mexico that just brings out the creative chef in me.

It also brings out my inner rebel and romantic. Hot Mexican passion. Something in the sangria, I guess. I distinctly remember the first time I made this meal , because it was followed by an absolutely amazing night of drunken skinny-dipping with my lover. Who could've guessed that sangria and tortilla soup would be the magical combination to pick my lover's locks?

Try it on your lover. Light a mango scented candle. Imagine. Cancun. Sangria. Chicken Vino Tortilla Soup. Prepare to be blown away. How could you go wrong with chicken, bacon, and Mexican spices?

FREE BONUS: The Smashed Chef's Unique and Intuitive Wine Pairing Guide, Filled with Gourmet Tips & Tricks. *www.lovesharecook.com/smashed-chef.*

Ingredients

3 cups chicken stock
⅓ cup dry red wine
1 pound chicken tenders
1 bay leaf, fresh if available1 tablespoon extra-virgin olive oil, 1 turn of the pan
4 slices thick, smoky center cut bacon, chopped
1 onion, finely chopped
4 cloves garlic, chopped
2 chipotles in adobo, chopped, plus 2 tablespoons sauce
1 28-ounce can crushed fire roasted tomatoes
Salt
4 cups lightly crushed corn tortilla chips
2 cups shredded fresh Smoked Mozzarella or Sharp White Cheddar Cheese,
1 lime, cut into wedges
½ red onion, chopped
Freshly chopped cilantro leaves, for garnish

Preparation

I don't care if you don't like sangria. Drink some. Okay, fine, red wine will also do fine. Just know that you're not going skinny-dipping tonight with *that* attitude.

- Put the broth and wine in a soup pot and simmer, covered. Poach the chicken tenders with bay leaf for 6-7 minutes.

- In a medium pot, put in olive oil over medium high heat. Cook bacon until crisp and remove from pot using a fork or slotted spoon to drain the oil. Keep only about 2-3 tablespoons of oil in pan.

- Now, put the garlic and onions into medium pot, sautéing for five minutes. Then stir in the chipotle peppers and tomatoes.

- Take your chicken out of the liquid and chop it up. Put it into the soup. Put the stock and wine mixture through a strainer, and then add to your pot. Layer the crushed tortillas chips in bottom of individual serving bowls. Cover with a handful of smoked cheese and ladle the soup on top. Garnish with lime, cilantro leaves, and some raw onions.

- Serve with wine or Corona beer with lime. While eating, casually, mention a skinny dip in the tub tonight. Smooth.

CHEESEBURGER CHEESEBURGER BEER SOUP

COOK TIME: 60 MINUTES

"You'll shoot your eye out, kid." Many of you may recognize the classic Christmas Story line referring to main character Ralphie's possession of a BB gun.

Well at twenty-five, I became Ralphie. Brand new BB gun, plenty of ammo, and a stockpile of liquor to make a lush blush. I'd brought five friends over to mess around with the gun. It wasn't a *real* gun, and I didn't think I could be trusted with one. After all, I was ,(as someone who wasn't raised in America) still pretty nervous that I'd shoot myself.

Unfortunately, it started raining just as my last friend arrived. Not to worry! Plenty of alcohol to be consumed, rain or shine. It would be just like a normal night amongst good friends. Like all great mistakes, however, the alcohol only served as a catalyst to our eventual plans. Drinking whiskey, posing like a cowboy in my living room, *Once Upon a Time in the West* playing on the TV—I suddenly had one of my "ideas." I'd make a target out of cardboard, put it on the wall, and we could just shoot at the cardboard!

My friends, reminiscent of the great betrayer Judas, agreed enthusiastically. I suppose I can't blame them; they were just as drunk as I was. Let's just say I didn't get my security deposit back. There are probably still BBs lodged in that wall, so I'd like to just quickly and publicly apologize to whoever rented the apartment after me.

This soup is the most American meal I've ever made. I love America. I love beer. I love burgers. One night I drunkenly decided that all of these things would make a great soup together. You know what? Drunken me is a genius.

FREE BONUS: The Smashed Chef's Unique and Intuitive Wine Pairing Guide, Filled with Gourmet Tips & Tricks. *www.lovesharecook.com/smashed-chef.*

41

Ingredients

⅔ pound ground chuck
½ teaspoon ground coriander
½ teaspoon ground cumin
½ teaspoon powdered garlic
½teaspoon dried minced onions
½ teaspoon salt
¼ teaspoon freshly ground black pepper
⅓ cup sharp cheddar cheese, grated
3 tablespoon olive oil, divided
1 medium onion, diced
¼ cup carrots, finely diced
¼ cup celery finely diced
¾ cup finely milled flour (such as Wondra brand) or all-purpose flour
1½ cups half and half
12 oz. beer (dark if you like it rich, lager if you prefer less beer flavor)
2 cups chicken stock
2 teaspoons Worcestershire sauce
8 ounces cheese, grated (strongly flavored cheeses, such as Sharp Cheddar,
     Gouda, Gruyere — a mix works well)
2 cups croutons, divided, for garnish

Preparation

■ Mix seasonings into ground chuck, but be sure you don't over
  work the mixture. Divide your meat in half, and smash each half
  into equal-sized rectangles on waxed paper. Make these as thin as
  you can but don't let them tear. Place the grated sharp cheddar
  over one rectangle. Gently lift the other rectangle and put it on
  top of your cheese-covered rectangle. Press firmly to seal them
  tight so your cheese does not leak too much. Place them in your
  freezer for 12-15 minutes to firm.

■ Heat 1 tablespoon olive oil in large skillet over medium heat.
  Remove cheeseburger rectangles from freezer and cut into small
  cheeseburger cheeseburger squares (around ¾"). When your oil
  shimmers, add half of the cheeseburger cheeseburger squares into
  your hot pan and cook them throughout. Remove your delicious
  cheeseburger cheeseburger squares to a double paper-towel lined
  plate to rest. Then cook up the other half.

- Warm the remaining 2 tablespoons olive oil in a 5-quart Dutch oven or stock pot over medium heat. When the oil shimmers, add the onions, carrots, and celery. Sauté until soft, about 6-8 minutes. Add the flour evenly and stir it in well to thoroughly coat the vegetables. Cook for two full minutes so you avoid a raw flour flavor. Pour in the half and half, ½ cup at a time, stirring constantly to thicken. You have made a roux. Keep tabs on the roux until it bubbles gently.

- Next, turn your heat to medium-high. Add the magical beer to your pan and stir well until all of the foam collapses and the soup returns to a slow simmer. Add the chicken stock and Worcestershire sauce, and then bring to a medium boil. Return the heat to medium—your soup should stay at a gentle bubble.

- Add the remaining cheese slowly, stirring well after each addition until it is completely incorporated into the soup. Then taste and season with salt and freshly ground pepper if you desire. Add your cheeseburger cheeseburger squares to the pot. Reduce the heat to low and cook for 10 minutes longer. Be patient. If you're ravenous, sample one of the cheeseburger cheeseburger squares...but be careful, they are habit forming (speaking from experience).

- Divide the croutons evenly in your soup bowls and ladle your amazing Cheeseburger Cheeseburger Beer Soup over the top of them.

- Amazing that all those meaty and cheesy ingredients made a soup that tastes just like baseball and apple pie.

FREE BONUS: The Smashed Chef's Unique and Intuitive Wine Pairing Guide, Filled with Gourmet Tips & Tricks. *www.lovesharecook.com/smashed-chef.*

43

QUICK FRENCH ONION SHERRY SOUP

COOK TIME: 30 MINUTES

Note: I, the Smashed Chef, do *not* recommend skiing drunk. Don't be the next Sonny Bono. That's what the cabin or ski lodge is for.

My friends and I tend to get highly competitive when drinking. Sometimes there's a healthy outlet for that tension. Other times there's nothing to do and all that's left is shenanigans. Such was the case on the night of the naked ski lodge.

The rules were simple: strip naked and see how long you can stay outside in a snowstorm. We got good and liquored up and then exited our nice, warm premises into the harsh and eerily quiet blizzard. With the amount of anti-freeze we had in our systems it didn't even feel cold. At first...

I'd love to say I won, for posterity, but I did not. I'd love to say I even came close to first place, but that also would be a lie. However, I can say I was not the first to crack. That would have been Andre. The shrinkage just horrified him.

Everyone appreciated I had the forethought to put a big pot of this soup on before we went outside, though. Nothing better than a steaming bowl of French onion soup on a cold day, and the additional sherry makes this recipe even more effective.

Ingredients

1 tablespoon extra-virgin olive oil
2 tablespoons butter
6 medium onions, thinly sliced
Salt and freshly ground black pepper to taste
2 teaspoons fresh thyme, picked and chopped or poultry seasoning
1 bay leaf, fresh or dried
½ cup dry sherry
6 cups beef stock
4 thick slices crusty bread, toasted
2½ cups shredded Gruyere or Swiss Cheese

Preparation

I'm about to save you hours this night. Hours you don't have for cooking. Hours you would rather use for drinking. Pour yourself a glass of wine and let's get going.

- Heat a large soup pot on medium high. Add the butter and oil to the pot and throw in the onions as you are slicing them. Add the salt and pepper and a teaspoon of fresh thyme. Let the onions cook 15 minutes to bring out their magic.

- By now, they should be partially caramelized. Throw in a bay leaf and the sherry to remove the glaze from the pan drippings (that's where the flavor is). Then add 6 cups of stock and boil quickly.

- Put 4 serving bowls on a baking sheet. When soup boils, put it in bowls and allow toasted bread to float on soup. Cover with cheese and thyme. Broil until cheese is bubbly and melted.

- Ten minutes. That's how long the winner lasted. Yeah, my friends are wimps.

FREE BONUS: The Smashed Chef's Unique and Intuitive Wine Pairing Guide, Filled with Gourmet Tips & Tricks. *www.lovesharecook.com/smashed-chef.*

45

SAUSAGE, WHITE BEAN AND BROCCOLI SOUP

COOK TIME: 30 MINUTES

It was Chicago where I had the most confusing drug-related encounter of my life. I'd been out at a club with my client all night, and it's safe to say that both of us were—how do you say it? Drunk. Drunk off eight-dollar beers and twelve-dollar mixed drinks, but drunk nonetheless.

To get back to where we were staying, unfortunately, we had accidentally walked across the wrong side of the tracks. Picture us: two unwitting, drunken idiots (or geniuses) traipsing down a street in the projects at two in the morning, laughing all the way. Then, picture my surprise when a giant mountain of a man emerges from the shadows to my immediate right, silhouetted against a single porch-light.

"Hey, you guys wanna buy some Mary Jane?" he growls.

"What?" I stammer back.

"Marijuana. You want some?" The man leans forward, threateningly.

"Uh...no, we're good, thanks." I laugh, nervously.

And then, as if the man's personality had changed entirely, he said, "Alright, gentlemen, you guys have a safe and fun night," and he disappeared back into the shadows. Friendly Rasta man? Undercover cop? I may never know.

Still, it was on this same trip in Chicago that I came up with a use for all the delicious sausage in that city. This Sausage, White Bean, and Broccoli Soup will have you yearning for long nights in the Windy City.

Smashed Chef Secrets: 3 Ways to Make Cooking More FUN!
1- Use your cooking time as a way to express your infinite creativity.
2- Use recipes for inspiration instead of getting stressed out if you are missing an ingredient. Your variation may be glorious!
3- Be satisfied with simple foods that don't take long to cook, yet taste delicious.

46

Ingredients

2 tablespoons extra-virgin olive oil, 2 turns of the pan
1¼ pounds Italian bulk sweet sausage
1 medium onion, chopped
¼ cup sherry
1 carrot, chopped
1 large potato, peeled and chopped into small dice
2 cloves garlic, chopped
1 bay leaf
2 15½ ounce cans white beans, drained
Salt and pepper
4 cups chopped broccoli rabe and greens
2 quarts chicken stock
Grated Parmigiano-Reggiano or Romano Cheese, to pass at table

Preparation

White or red wine goes well with this soup. Go ahead, pour yourself a glass.

- Heat your soup pot on medium to high heat. Put in olive oil and brown the sausage. Add the vegetables, beans, and bay leaf. Cook for about five minutes to soften vegetables. Add the rabe and allow it to wilt. Add sherry and stock to the soup and let boil. Reduce heat to a simmer and cook, uncovered, for 15 minutes. Serve with grated cheese on top.

- Stay away from back alleys. If someone harasses you, bribe them with this soup. Sorry, it's the best advice I have.

FREE BONUS: The Smashed Chef's Unique and Intuitive Wine Pairing Guide, Filled with Gourmet Tips & Tricks. *www.lovesharecook.com/smashed-chef.*

47

CHARDONNAY CHICKEN STEW

COOK TIME: 50 MINUTES

Not much to this one. One of my Hollywood clients, a film producer I'll call "John" from here on out, had a penchant for fast cars. One night he asked me to go out driving with him on Pacific Coast Highway. For those that don't know, Pacific Coast Highway (or PCH from here on out) resembles a big, twisted piece of spaghetti. Think of a road entirely made of hairpin turns.

John decided to drive this road at night, going double the speed limit, with me screaming in the passenger's seat. Not "screaming" in a figurative sense, but literally screaming as we went around certain turns. (Of course he was stone sober, but I had a pretty good buzz going...) Had there been a car coming in the opposite direction on some of those turns, we'd be dead. Have you ever been so sure that you were going to die that you texted your friend some last minute additions to your will? Because I have.

I sat there imagining my death in a thousand different ways: flying off a cliff, hitting another car, or just having a heart attack. I promised that if I made it out alive, I'd come up with a new recipe so I could get rid of the rest of my Chardonnay.

You're lucky I survived, readers. This is that near-death recipe, and it's delicious. The wine-infused chicken stew is done in under an hour, but it will taste like you slaved away all day. Just do me a favor: stay in bed after you eat instead of driving like a maniac down PCH.

Ingredients

2 tablespoons olive oil
2 stalks celery, cut into bite-size pieces
1 carrot, peeled, cut into bite-size pieces
1 small onion, chopped
½ cup Chardonnay
Salt and freshly ground black pepper
1 14½-ounce can chopped tomatoes
1 14-ounce can low-salt chicken broth
½ cup fresh basil leaves, torn into pieces
1 tablespoon tomato paste
1 bay leaf
½ teaspoon dried thyme leaves
2 chicken breast with ribs (about 1 ½ pounds total)
1 15-ounce can organic kidney beans, drained (rinsed if not organic)

Preparation

This dish takes a little longer than 40 minutes. Pour a glass of Chardonnay and deal with it.

- Use a large saucepan on medium heat. Put in the carrots, celery, and onion. Sauté these vegetables for approximately 5 minutes. Add salt and pepper to taste. Then add Chardonnay, tomatoes, basil, chicken broth, tomato paste, thyme, and the bay leaf. Bring to a simmer. Gently place in the chicken breasts into the pot, and cook for about 20 minutes.

- Remove the chicken pieces from the broth and allow them to cool briefly while getting rid of the bay leaf. Put the beans in the pot and allow the stew to thicken for about 10 minutes. Remove and shred all the juicy meat from the skin and bones before returning it to the stew. Finalize your spices after a taste.

- Serve stew in large bowls and crusty bread on the side.

FREE BONUS: The Smashed Chef's Unique and Intuitive Wine Pairing Guide, Filled with Gourmet Tips & Tricks. *www.lovesharecook.com/smashed-chef.*

49

SPAGHETTI AND MEAT-A-BALLA SOUPY STEW

COOK TIME: 42 MINUTES

Right around the time I made my Cheeseburger Cheeseburger Beer Soup, I got into a phase where I just wanted to make everything into a soup. I don't know why. Perhaps it was winter. Or maybe I was tired of having to chew my food. Or perchance my fondness for drinking made me think I should *drink* everything. Of course it could have been the alcohol itself that made this seem like a great idea.

Actually, yes, it was just the alcohol that made this seem like a great idea. I imagine the process is a lot like making oddly-flavored jelly beans. "Why should we make a grass flavored jelly bean? Well, why not?!"

Unfortunately, soup is not as versatile as jelly beans, and many of these experiments were failures. I would not recommend, for instance, making a soup out of your Thanksgiving stuffing. However, this Spaghetti and Meat-a-Balla Soupy Stew is incredible. It's all the things you love about a great spaghetti, except easier! The secret is the chicken stock base; otherwise the soup would be more stew than soup. Now it's soupy stew. Perfecto.

Ingredients

2 tablespoons extra virgin olive oil
1 carrot, peeled and chopped into a small dice
1 medium yellow skinned onion, chopped
2 small ribs celery from the heart, chopped
3 cloves garlic, chopped
3 cups tomato sauce or 1 14-ounce can plus 1 8-ounce can
3 cups chicken stock, available in a box on the soup aisle
3 cups Chardonnay or other dry white wine
1 pound ground beef, pork and veal mix (meatloaf mix) available at butcher counter
½ cup grated cheese, Parmigianino or Romano, plus more to pass at table
½ cup Italian bread crumbs
1 large egg, beaten
2 tablespoons chopped parsley leaves
½ pound spaghetti, broken in half
1 cup basil leaves, torn or shredded
1 loaf Italian crusty bread, for dunking

Preparation

Bring forth the vino! Enjoy a glass and let's get cracking...

- Heat up your soup pot over medium heat. Add olive oil along with onions, carrots, celery, and garlic. Sauté these for five minutes.
- Now add the Chardonnay and tomato sauce. Add the stock and cover your pot. Bring to a brisk boil and reduce heat to low.
- Now mix the meat, cheese, bread crumbs, parsley, and eggs together, forming meat-a-ballas with them. Make them the size of a large marble, small enough to easily eat in one bite. Put meat-a-ballas in soup and bring back to boil. Add spaghetti and then turn down to simmer, covered, for 10 more minutes or until meat-a-ballas are cooked and pasta is soft.
- Stir in the basil and serve with cheese and crusty bread.

As for those failed attempts? Imagine the spaghetti and meat-a-ballas equivalent of baby food.

FREE BONUS: The Smashed Chef's Unique and Intuitive Wine Pairing Guide, Filled with Gourmet Tips & Tricks. *www.lovesharecook.com/smashed-chef.*

51

AUTUMN PUMPKIN SOUP

COOK TIME: 40 MINUTES

I love living in Idaho. It's a great base to return to after a couple of weeks partying, because everything moves at a much healthier pace. Still, when I tell people where I live I invariably get a single response.

"Idaho? So like, you get good potatoes right?"

For your information, hypothetical inquisitor, we also get great apples and pumpkins here, among other delicacies. This soup will help you unwind after running all day and night at breakneck speed. In other words, it will help you get rid of last night's hangover. Let yourself enjoy the rich tastes of autumn, just for one day. The booze and the parties will be there again tomorrow.

I use canned pumpkin puree in this recipe now because fresh pumpkin takes far too long, but the apples and other raw ingredients ensures that it still tastes vibrantly fresh. It goes great with Oktoberfest beer too.

Ingredients

1 tablespoon extra-virgin olive oil,
2 tablespoons butter
1 fresh bay leaf
2 ribs celery with greens, finely chopped
1 medium yellow onion, finely chopped
½ cup dry white wine
Salt and pepper to taste
3 tablespoons all-purpose flour
2 teaspoons poultry seasoning or 2 teaspoons ground thyme
2 teaspoons hot sauce, or to taste
6 cups chicken stock
1 28-ounce can cooked pumpkin puree
2 cups heavy cream
½ teaspoon freshly grated nutmeg

Relish

1 crisp apple, such as McIntosh or Granny Smith, finely chopped
¼ red onion, finely chopped
2 tablespoons lemon juice
½ cup dried sweetened cranberries, chopped
1 teaspoon chili powder
2 teaspoons honey
½ teaspoon ground cinnamon

Preparation

- Heat your soup pot on medium heat. Add oil and butter along with celery, bay leaf, onion, and white wine. Salt and pepper veggies to taste. Let veggies cook 6-7 minutes or until soft.

- Now mix in flour, hot sauce, and poultry seasoning. Whisk the chicken stock into mixture and let it bubble. Using a whisk, add the pumpkin slowly and lovingly. Simmer uncovered for about 10 minutes or until soup thickens.

- Mix in nutmeg and cream, reducing heat to low, until ready to serve. Serve warm with relish. To make the relish, mix the onion, apple, cranberries, lemon juice, honey, cinnamon, and chili powder. Put on top of the soup.

FREE BONUS: The Smashed Chef's Unique and Intuitive Wine Pairing Guide, Filled with Gourmet Tips & Tricks. *www.lovesharecook.com/smashed-chef.*

53

SPICY BEER BINGE CHILI

COOK TIME: 2 HOURS

They say, "Drink responsibly," and I could not fulfill that maxim if I neglected to include a great chili recipe. Even though this recipe takes a bit longer to cook, you'll appreciate it. Plus, it's only twenty minutes of prep time.

Now, in most of these introductions, I tell you a story about myself. I like to think I've led a pretty crazy life, and I hope you find these anecdotes amusing as you peruse my recipes. Occasionally, though, someone else has a story *so unbelievable* that I feel it would be a disservice to include my own tale instead of theirs. Such is the case with chili.

I bet you didn't know that chili killed a man. That's right. In 2008, a man died after consuming super-hot chili. He and a friend had made a bet about who could make the spiciest dish, and the aspiring chef used a batch of home-grown red chilies to make the hottest sauce he possibly could. The next morning he was dead, and investigators were forced to blame it on the chili.

As far as I know, this chili has never caused any deaths; it's nowhere near as spicy. In fact, I'd dare say it's a perfect blend of ingredients and spice, though I'm certainly biased. There's no greater pairing than chili and beer, so crack open a cold one and enjoy a hot bowl.

Ingredients

3 tablespoons canola oil

¾ lb. ground chili ground beef (A course grind. Use regular ground beef as a substitute if necessary)

¾ lb. ground pork

½ lb. sirloin cut into small cubes

2 large white onions, chopped medium fine

2 14½ -ounce cans diced tomatoes

2 15-ounce cans tomato sauce

2 12-ounce cans dark beer

2 15-ounce cans spicy chili beans, un-drained

¼ cup Worcestershire sauce

3 tablespoons Tabasco sauce

2 tablespoons ancho chili powder (May substitute regular chili powder, but you'll the miss deeper flavor)

4 tablespoons regular chili powder

4 fresh jalapeno peppers, seeded and chopped

3 tablespoons red pepper flakes (Adjust to taste, or eliminate if you don't like much heat)

Celtic sea salt to taste

Sour cream, for garnish (optional)

Cotija cheese, for garnish (optional)

Cilantro, for garnish (optional)

Tortilla chips, for garnish (optional)

Preparation

- Lightly oil a Dutch oven with 1 tablespoon of canola oil. Brown the cubed up sirloin over medium high heat very quickly. Take out after it's seared. Remove and dispose of any juices. Smashed Chef Cooking Secret: Always cook meat like this in SMALL batches. Too much meat means too much moisture. You don't want boiled meat.

- Add 1 tablespoon of canola oil and the ground pork and cook. Remove and put in bowl with cooked cubes of beef. Remove and dispose of any juices from Dutch oven. Add 1 tablespoon of canola oil and cook the chili ground meat, stirring occasionally until evenly browned. Drain and dispose of juices one more time.

- Now, add the other meats to the browned chili ground beef in the Dutch oven. Add the onion, diced tomatoes, tomato sauce, beer, and chili beans. Season up with chili powder, jalapenos, Worcestershire sauce, red pepper flakes and salt to taste.

FREE BONUS: The Smashed Chef's Unique and Intuitive Wine Pairing Guide, Filled with Gourmet Tips & Tricks. *www.lovesharecook.com/smashed-chef.*

55

- Cover the Dutch oven and simmer over low heat for 2 hours. Stir occasionally.
- Eat now, or refrigerate for a day or two to let the flavors meld even more. (That's what I do.)
- Garnish with sour cream, Cotija cheese, cilantro and/or tortilla chips if you like.

Food brings us together. And no one is more revered than the cook. You don't have to be a chef to be adored. All you need to do is add the secret ingredient of love.

These booze-infused main dishes will make you a star. They will add life to each dinner conversation and intensify your connections. Yes, food helps create moments.

SMASHING SPAGHETTI A LA CARBONARA

COOK TIME: 25 MINUTES

I share my favorite pasta dish first. It is simple to prepare and delectable to eat. It is a dish for lovers and friends alike. They will sing your praises and request this dish over and over again. Like my lady does...

I remember cooking it the first time for my lover. As she walked into the small house I was renting, I became flush with excitement. I poured her a glass of a fine Pinot Grigio to set the mood, lit candles on a table with a red checkered table cloth and gazed into her deep azure eyes.

Yes, it was a magical moment we would never forget. I handed her my old photo album full of pictures my family had taken in the 1970's. We lived in Tuscany and I regaled her with stories of the *Giro d'Italia* passing our home... of skiing in the Dolomites... and of life at a slow, measured pace. All while preparing the pasta with a love and devotion she had never seen before. In under 30 minutes, we dined.

That was the night that sealed our love in time. Forever. We retired afterward and danced the dance of lovers. I left her undisturbed in the morning. A note on the night stand with prose was left behind. Spoken words could not covey my emotions... and a jet awaited me.

Carbonara in America is an outrage. They add creams that do not belong in a classic preparation of this dish. The rustic Carbonara prepared in Italian farm homes will show you how simple and elegant this dish can be.

Unlike the imposter recipes you find all over the Interwebz, this recipe has a pedigree. It was taught to me by the little old Italian grandmother who taught me how to make meat-a-ballas.

Pasta is love Mon Cheri. Don't ever forget it. You can create emotions and feelings with a simple pasta dish that fill volumes of books.

Ingredients

1 pound dry spaghetti (I prefer whole wheat as it has much more of a nutty flavor)
2 tablespoons extra-virgin olive oil
4 ounces pancetta or slab bacon, cut into strips
5 garlic cloves, finely chopped
2 large eggs
1 cup freshly grated Parmigiano-Reggiano, plus more for serving
Freshly ground black pepper
1 cup fresh flat-leaf parsley, chopped and loosely packed
½ cup dry white wine

Preparation

- First, put a pot of salted water on the stove over high heat to prepare the spaghetti.
- As it heats to a boil, warm a deep skillet over medium heat. Place in olive oil, warm it and add the pancetta or bacon. Sauté about 5 minutes until the fat renders and the pork becomes crispy. Take out pancetta or bacon and reserve in a paper towel lined bowl. Turn off heat.
- When your pot is boiling, add your spaghetti. Cook for the lowest time on the package to make sure your spaghetti is done al dente. If it says 8-10 minutes, test it at 7, cook no longer than 8. (This is a critical step. Your lover will not appreciate mushy pasta. And I know you love things firm...)
- While pasta is cooking, have a sip of your wine and get your eggs and cheese. Mix the eggs and cheese with a whisk. Stir out all of the lumps. That's it, very good. Set aside.
- Warm your rendered pancetta or bacon fat. When warm, about 2 minutes, add the chopped garlic. Take off heat.
- By now your pasta should be cooked al dente. Drain thoroughly, set aside some of the liquid. (½ cup).
- Add the pasta to your deep skillet full of rendered fat and garlic. Add the egg and cheese mixture and mix in rapidly for about 2 minutes, so the mixture thickens quickly and your eggs do not get scrambled (they will still cook, the hot pasta will cook them).

- Add the wine, and if needed, add some of the reserved pasta liquid to thin the sauces. Mix in reserved pancetta or bacon, along with most of your parsley. Garnish with more fresh parsley and more bacon if you desire.

- Pile this into a family style bowl and serve with a salad and crusty bread. This is perfect for a bottle of Pinot Grigio. Pass the cheese...

FREE BONUS: The Smashed Chef's Unique and Intuitive Wine Pairing Guide, Filled with Gourmet Tips & Tricks. *www.lovesharecook.com/smashed-chef.*

59

MOMMA'S LASAGNA AND MUSHROOMS
MADE QUICK!

COOK TIME: 70 MINUTES

Yes, I see that the cook time is 70 minutes. But it only takes around 15 minutes to prepare before baking. Sensuous lasagna for you and your lover in a tad over an hour. That is truly a miracle... even for the Smashed Chef.

I first created this quick version while sailing near the Aleutian Islands in the summer of 1991. A client who was a founder of a huge software company at the time asked me to be his private chef aboard his sailboat, a 63' Gulfstar Sailcruiser. My order for food provisions had arrived on the ship in Seattle. I was not there to check it. The day I had lasagna on the menu, I noticed that whoever shopped for the lasagna noodles had made an error and bought no-cook noodles.

At first I was enraged. But then, I saw this was a gift. You see this particular client was very needy. He had me jumping at every whim he could think up. I had no time to write letters the whole trip... until that fateful day.

I locked myself in the galley, made noises of crashing pots and pans for hours. But during that time I wrote 7 letters. And I made the lasagna in under an hour. My finicky software nerd couldn't tell the difference.

This recipe puts a new twist on lasagna by adding hot Italian sausage and baby mushrooms. It's a quick recipe because it makes use of no cook lasagna noodles and premade sausage with its casing removed. (Also known as bulk sausage.) It's a great meal to serve your lover any time of the year, but especially as it gets colder and you need more snuggling time.

Smashed Chef Secrets: *Similar to "instant rice," no-cook lasagna noodles are pre-cooked by the manufacturer. Noodles are prepared and then mechanically dried. While baking, the noodles rehydrate with the moisture in the lasagna sauce.*

60

Ingredients

2 tablespoons olive oil

2 8-ounce packages sliced crimini mushrooms

1 large onion, chopped (about 2 cups)

2 tablespoons dried Italian seasoning blend

1 pound hot Italian sausages, casings removed

3 garlic cloves, pressed

1 cup dry red wine

$4^2/_3$ cups marinara sauce (from two 26-ounce jars)

1 9-ounce package no-cook lasagna noodles

1 15-ounce container ricotta cheese

2 8-ounce bags Italian blend grated cheese

Preparation

Go to the kitchen 2 hours before cooking and thrash pots and pans about. Your lover will think you are slaving away, whilst you are really drinking wine. Come back from time to time and repeat. An hour before dinner return and let's cook.

- Set your oven to 400 F. Using a large pot, heat the oil with mushrooms, onions and seasonings. Sauté for about 6 minutes. Then sauté the sausage until cooked completely through for about 5 minutes. The sausage should be in small pieces. Put in garlic for an additional minute. Next add wine and cook for about two minutes and lay aside.

- To make lasagna, spread $^2/_3$ cup of marinara sauce on the bottom of a 9 x 13 pan. Lay out a layer of noodles down and then ricotta and grated cheese. (I like using the straight no-cook noodles.) Finally add sausage. Continue doing these layers until the top of the pan is reached, finishing with grated cheese.

- Use foil for the top and "tent" it so it doesn't touch your precious cheese. Bake under foil for 45 minutes. Remove foil and allow top to brown and bubble for 10 more minutes. Set for 15 minutes to meld flavors and cool.

- Enjoy with a Caesar salad and a dry red wine.

Write a letter to an old friend with all of the time you saved. Make it a "snail mail" letter. Be old fashioned, it's a lost art. Then snuggle with your lover. That's a lost art too.

FREE BONUS: The Smashed Chef's Unique and Intuitive Wine Pairing Guide, Filled with Gourmet Tips & Tricks. *www.lovesharecook.com/smashed-chef.*

61

SOUSED SPAGHETTI WITH SEAFOOD

COOK TIME: 30 MINUTES

It's a splendid Italian tradition to have the Feast of the Seven Fishes on Christmas Eve. But you'll desire this dish all year round. It is packed with the flavor of the sea.

While scouting the Mediterranean coast of Italy, looking for a place for us to live, my mother discovered seafood pasta. In a very small restaurant a few blocks from the ocean, she could smell the wonderful aroma of seafood and wine. She ordered a simple seafood pasta, packed with clams and mussels. She was very persistent with the waiter, begging to tour the kitchen and soon the owner/chef came to the table.

He seemed delighted by my mother's broken Italian and invited her back to see the goings on. The chef poured her a glass of wine and told her of the tradition of the Feast of the Seven Fishes. An order came in for the seafood pasta and my mother studied his simple techniques to prepare this wonderful dish.

We moved to that city a week before Christmas. Our first Feast of the Seven Fishes featured this amazing dish. And now I share it with you.

Ingredients

20-24 clams
20-24 mussels
1 pound spaghetti
¼ cup extra-virgin olive oil
¼ cup Pinot Grigio
4 cloves garlic, shaved paper thin
½ cup calamari, sliced
16 pieces shrimp
1 teaspoon crushed red pepper

Preparation

This dish is very simple, very quick to prepare. Turn on some music, pour a glass of wine and let's cook.

- First, cook the clams and mussels with ½ cup water in a covered pan until cooked. The shells should open. If they do not, discard them. Reserve the liquid. Remove the meat from inside of the clams and mussels. Dispose of the shells.
- In boiling salted water, begin cooking the spaghetti.
- Simultaneously, heat up the extra-virgin olive oil on medium-high heat in a large sauté pan. Add the crushed red pepper and shaved garlic and slowly sauté. Just when the edges of the garlic become slightly browned, take the pan off the heat and add 1 cup of your reserved pasta cooking water to your pan. Put it back on the heat, keeping it on medium high.
- When the pasta is three-quarters of the way cooked, remove from the boiling water to the sauté pan. Reserve the cooking liquid in case you need it later.
- Continue cooking the spaghetti in the sauté pan using the reserved pasta cooking water to thin more, if needed (only use a tiny bit at a time, do not make too liquidy). Add more clam and mussel liquid if you want more creaminess. Just before the pasta is cooked, add the cooked clams and mussels, squid, and shrimp. Finish cooking the pasta with all the seafood until al dente.
- Remove the seafood pasta and place in a serving bowl. Serve immediately.

THREE SHEETS TO THE WIND MUSSELS

COOK TIME: 20 MINUTES

Just 2 weeks ago, one of my friends returned from a business trip to Seattle. As he sometimes does, (when he feels the urge to invite himself for a meal), he brings me an offering of seafood from the World Famous Pike Place Market. This time it was fresh mussels.

Of course you don't bring mussels as a gift and store them for long. As soon as my eyes beheld those jewels of the sea, I had to prepare them that night. My friend joined me in the kitchen and we talked as I cooked. I also made him honorary sous chef... so I got to order him around, which is always a treat. (He's a hard charging businessman, not used to taking orders. I delight in mercilessly bossing him!)

That is how you can make cooking more fun. Invite a friend to chat as you cook. Put that friend to work as your assistant and boss him or her around. The kitchen is your domain tonight. And you shall laugh the belly laugh of friendship.

The white wine and garlic sauce perks up the meaty, oceany mussels in this dish. It's one of my favorite ways to enjoy mussels.

Ingredients

4 qts. fresh mussels
1 16-oz. pkg. linguine pasta
3 Tbs. butter
1 onion, chopped
2 cloves garlic, minced
6 Tbs. chopped fresh parsley
1 bay leaf
¼ teaspoon. dried thyme
2 C. white wine

Preparation

Do you have a sous chef to boss around tonight? It's a good night to have one.

- Get them scrubbing the mussels and pull off their beards. Then cutting them at the base with a stout paring knife. Throw away the ones that do not close when you handle them and of course any with broken shells.
- Bring a large pot of salted water to a rolling boil. Add your pasta and cook until al dente (go on the short side of the pasta Preparation). Drain and set the pasta aside.
- Now, in a 12 inch skillet, put 2 tablespoons butter, onion, garlic, bay leaf, parsley, thyme and finally the wine. Bring this mixture to a boil and lower heat. Cook for 2 to 3 minutes.
- Add the mussels still in the shells. Cover the pan and cook until they open, 3 to 4 minutes at the most. Do not overcook the jewels of the sea.
- Divide your pasta evenly into 4 bowls and spoon mussels over your linguine, while reserving mussel liquid. (We chefs call this liquor... no, not just me.)
- Strain the mussel liquid, and return to your pot. Add all of the remaining butter and heat through until it melts. Pour over your lovely mussels and serve immediately.

That didn't even take long enough to thoroughly enjoy bossing your friend around. Maybe you should invite them over again soon. Toast your creation and enjoy friendship.

Smashed Chef Secrets: Plan your menu so you get plenty of time to prepare the dish, plus the time to prepare yourself and your eating area. Being stressed out due to lack of time will not set the ambiance you desire for romance!

FREE BONUS: The Smashed Chef's Unique and Intuitive Wine Pairing Guide, Filled with Gourmet Tips & Tricks. *www.lovesharecook.com/smashed-chef.*

65

LEMON WINE GNOCCHI

COOK TIME: 20 MINUTES

I love the luxuriousness of gnocchi. They are like light little pasta dumplings. In Italy, they are served as a first course. But I like them so much, any course can be a gnocchi course! (Yes, even dessert...)

You can find dried gnocchi in the pasta aisle of any gourmet grocery. I used to make it by hand, but when I'm in a rush to feed a group of friends, I don't mind taking shortcuts. They rarely ever notice. It makes for a fabulously quick entree that will satisfy hearty appetites.

The zing of fresh lemon enhances both the peas' sweetness and the natural flavor of the spinach. The whole quick, creamy dish is bolstered by soft pillows of potato gnocchi.

Ingredients

1 cup frozen baby peas (not thawed)
½ cup heavy cream
¼ Cup White Wine
¼teaspoon dried hot red-pepper flakes
1 garlic clove, smashed
3 cups packed baby spinach (3 ounces)
1 teaspoon grated lemon zest
1½ teaspoons fresh lemon juice
1 pound dried gnocchi (preferably De Cecco)
¼ cup grated parmesan

Smashed Chef Secrets: Al Dente pasta is digested more slowly and keeps blood sugar levels from spiking. It also helps you stay satisfied longer so you keep your svelte figure. ;-)

Preparation

- In a 12 inch skillet, simmer the frozen peas in your cream, red-pepper flakes, garlic, and season with ¼ teaspoon salt, covered, until tender, about 5 minutes.

- Next, add the spinach and simmer over medium-low heat, uncovered, while stirring, until the spinach is wilted. Remove from the burner and stir in the lemon zest and fresh lemon juice.

- Now, cook the gnocchi in a pot of boiling salted water until al dente. Do not overcook, it should be slightly chewy, but not hard inside. Reserve ¼ cup of your pasta cooking water, then drain the gnocchi in a strainer.

- Now for the magic. Add the cooked gnocchi to your sauce. Add the cheese and the wine plus some of your reserved cooking water, and stir to coat the gnocchi well. Thin with additional cooking water until it gets to a creamy consistency.

THE SMASHED CHEF'S VODKA SAUCE

COOK TIME: 75 MINUTES

Yes, I do promise easy to prepare recipes in 40 minutes or less. But sometimes The Smashed Chef must include recipes that take longer. Why? Because they are classic and delicious! And the prep time is short my busy lady. Most of the time is spent simmering and marrying flavors.

Vodka sauce has been a staple of mine since I became a professional chef. The vodka helps release the normally inaccessible flavors of tomato. (Although wine can do the same, vodka is unique!)

My drunken rock star client demands this decadently creamy sauce every time I accompany him on tour. It will become a favorite of yours too.

Ingredients

½ cup salted butter
1 cup vodka, plus 1 shot
1 large onion, diced
2 (28 ounce) cans crushed tomato
1 pint heavy cream

Preparation

- In a 12 inch skillet over medium heat, sauté your onion in butter until slightly brown and soft. (Just starting to caramelize.)
- Pour in vodka and let it simmer for 10 minutes.
- Mix in the crushed tomatoes and cook for another 30 minutes.
- Now pour in your heavy cream and cook for another 30 minutes.
- Serve with just about any pasta, cooked al dente. Cheers!

FREE BONUS: The Smashed Chef's Unique and Intuitive Wine Pairing Guide, Filled with Gourmet Tips & Tricks. *www.lovesharecook.com/smashed-chef.*

69

PLASTERED PASTA AL POMODORO

COOK TIME: 40 MINUTES

I love how simple Italians make cooking. You can literally feel their passion for food. Many chefs think they need to add 42 ingredients and take hours to make a good meal. But when they go out... simple dishes are what they crave.

A lovely pomodoro sauce is a marvel of simplicity. It's one of my go-to dishes to prepare on assignments from feeding hungry C-Level skier clients in Aspen to adventure junky "trust-funders" scuba diving in the warm South Pacific. It fuels high-adrenaline exploits and pleases the palate every time.

I created this simple pomodoro sauce in a yurt while snow-cat skiing in southern Alberta, Canada with a group 2 chef friends. (A yurt is a simple, portable, bent wood-framed "tent" traditionally used by nomads in the steppes of Central Asia, but is also used as fancy tent for outdoors people.) Wine was limited as we consumed our stores each night. Yet even with a small amount, it added a nice essence to the sauce.

It's bright, fresh flavor comes from the tomatoes and fresh basil. If it can be made in a yurt... your kitchen is a snap.

Ingredients

¼ cup extra-virgin olive oil
1 medium onion, minced
4 garlic cloves, minced
¼ cup of dry red wine
1 28 oz. can peeled tomatoes, puréed in a food processor
3 large fresh basil sprigs
12 oz. spaghetti
2 Tbs. cubed unsalted butter
1 pinch crushed red pepper flakes
Celtic Sea Salt
¼ cup finely grated Pecorino Romano

70

Preparation

- Drain ¼ cup of tomato liquid from the canned tomatoes. Put the tomatoes and remaining juice into a food processor. Add the wine. Process in food processor until pureed.

- In a large sauce pot, heat olive oil on medium low heat. Don't allow it to smoke. Add minced onion when oil shimmers. Sauté the onions and stir until soft, approximately 10 minutes. Add garlic and cook 2 or 3 minutes more. Now add the crushed red pepper flakes and cook 1 more minute.

- Increase the heat in this pan to medium. Add pureed tomato mixture to pot the along with olive oil, pepper flakes and garlic. Season to taste with Celtic sea salt. Cook lovingly until it thickens, about 15 minutes.

- Remove the pan from heat, stir in basil sprigs, and allow it to rest.

- In a large pot, bring salted water to a boil. Add your spaghetti and cook. Stir occasionally. Cook about 2 minutes less than pasta Preparation. Drain pasta and reserve ½ cup pasta cooking liquid.

- Discard basil from large cooking pot with sauce and heat up to high. Stir in reserved pasta water to loosen sauce (if necessary). Bring to a quick boil. Add your almost cooked pasta and cook, stirring, until sauce coats pasta and pasta is al dente, about 2 minutes.

- Remove your pot from the heat. Add a dollop of butter and be generous with the cheese. Toss until the cheese melts.

- Use tongs and place sauced pasta into warm bowls. Spoon any remaining sauce on top. Serve with more cheese and Chianti of course.

- Tomorrow you will be fully carbed up for that big day.

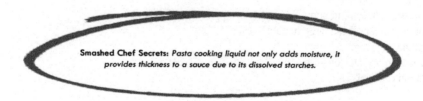

Smashed Chef Secrets: *Pasta cooking liquid not only adds moisture, it provides thickness to a sauce due to its dissolved starches.*

CROCKED CAPELLINI WITH PRAWNS

COOK TIME: 20 MINUTES

What is capellini? It's angel hair pasta, or as I call it – Goddess Hair. Many times this lovely pasta is sold in a nest-like shape. Very fun for days when your boss has worked your hands to the bone, and you want a quick gourmet meal. Was today like that?

It's time to escape into 20 minutes of cooking meditation today. It will help slow your frenetic pace of run, run, run. You deserve some time with your thoughts and the rhythm of cooking. It's another big day tomorrow, and capellini will fuel you as you climb the corporate ladder.

My very favorite way to prepare capellini is with seafood. They go together like a soup spoon and pint of Ben and Jerry's. My lady goes nuts for both, as long as chocolate is involved.

This is a very quick-cooking, yet seductive dish. Perfect for a day like today. Don't you agree?

Sweet vermouth intensifies the natural sweet flavor of tomatoes. The addition of cream gives it a silken quality. And best of all, it tastes like you've been simmering for hours. Hours I know you don't have.

Ingredients

3 tablespoons olive oil
1 pound peeled large prawns
3 large garlic cloves, forced through a garlic press
¼ teaspoon dried oregano
½ cup sweet (red) vermouth
1 (14- to 15-ounce) can diced tomatoes, drained
¾ cup heavy cream
½ teaspoon fresh lemon juice
½ pound capellini

Preparation

- In a large pot, heat salted water to boil for the pasta.
- While the water warms, in a separate 12 inch skillet, heat oil over medium high until shimmery. Add the prawns, oregano and garlic. Salt and pepper liberally. Turn prawns only once after about 1 minute. They should be golden when turned. Be careful, don't overcook. Cook about 1 more minute.
- Now add the vermouth, the tomatoes and scrape up the flavorful bits from the bottom of the pan. Pour in the cream and quickly simmer until the sauce gets thick and luxurious. About a minute or two. Stir in fresh lemon juice and turn off heat.
- Your water should be boiling. Add the pasta and cook until al dente. Capellini only takes 3-4 minutes. You'll disappoint yourself if you let it linger in the pot too long. Reserve ¾ cup of pasta liquid.
- Check your sauce for consistency. If too thick, add reserved pasta liquid until desired constancy.
- Serve in pre-warmed shallow bowls immediately. You shall be regaled as the goddess of the kitchen tonight.

Sometimes when The Smashed Chef is bored, he makes capellini just to PASTA time away.

FREE BONUS: The Smashed Chef's Unique and Intuitive Wine Pairing Guide, Filled with Gourmet Tips & Tricks. *www.lovesharecook.com/smashed-chef.*

73

SAUCED CALAMARI PASTA

COOK TIME: 35 MINUTES

My hard partying rock star client is Sicilian, and loves to visit his home every year. One year, he invited me along on his visit to Sicily, not as his private chef, but as his friend. Sicilians have such love. They treat you like long lost family.

After a few days of relaxing and eating amazing local foods prepared by his friends and family, I went on a solo excursion to the markets.

Palermo, Sicily is famous for its markets. And the fish markets are glorious. You have never seen such fresh, vibrant seafood. Some of it looks as if it could still swim away.

As I walked the aisles of the market, I spied a display of amazing looking calamari. I could not resist buying some and planned to prepare a special meal as my way of saying thanks.

That night, after much wine, I prepared this calamari pasta. We drank, we ate, and we laughed. Pasta is a party.

This dish is amazingly creamy. Linguine provides a canvas Michelangelo would approve of. It soaks up the flavors and provides an amazing textural contrast. And the spicy wine-basil-cream sauce is... well, my hosts said it best – *divino!*

Ingredients

½ pound linguine pasta
2 tablespoons olive oil
3 cloves garlic, crushed
8 ounces squid, cleaned and cut into rings and tentacles
¾ cup white wine
3 cherry peppers, thinly sliced
2 tablespoons cornstarch
1 cup cream
crushed red pepper flakes to taste
salt and pepper to taste
½ cup shredded fresh basil
¼ cup freshly grated Parmesan cheese

Preparation

If tonight you choose to unleash your *Inner Sicilian* a Chardonnay would suffice. They make a lovely Chardonnay and a sip will help you unwind. Are you ready to cook? Good.

- Bring a large pot of salted water to a rolling boil. Add pasta and cook for 8 to 10 minutes or until al dente (go on the shorter side, it will continue to cook a little). Drain it and set aside.

- Now heat your olive oil in a large skillet over medium-high heat. This will go very quick, but will seem as if you cooked all day. Add the crushed garlic and cook for a few seconds until it turns golden brown.

- Stir in your beautiful calamari and cook it until it turns white. Now pour in your white wine and put in the cherry pepper slices. Bring to a simmer and cook until the wine is reduced by about half. This should take approximately 3 minutes.

- Gently but firmly stir the cornstarch into the cream. Add it to your simmering calamari.

- Now season with basil, red pepper flakes. salt and pepper to taste. Stir until thickened just right.

- To serve, toss your pasta with sauce in your skillet. Place in a family style serving bowl and sprinkle generously with Parmesan cheese.

- Serve with a salad and bread. Pour the wine like a Sicilian--With gusto!

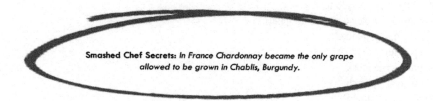

Smashed Chef Secrets: *In France Chardonnay became the only grape allowed to be grown in Chablis, Burgundy.*

FREE BONUS: The Smashed Chef's Unique and Intuitive Wine Pairing Guide, Filled with Gourmet Tips & Tricks. *www.lovesharecook.com/smashed-chef.*

75

TIPSY TURKEY AND SPINACH WITH PASTA

COOK TIME: 25 MINUTES

Yes, The Smashed Chef eats light a lot. He must keep his weight down so he may climb nasty hills on his bicycle. It's not just about cooking, one must have hobbies, don't you think? All work, work, work makes a dull chef.

{Switching back to 1st person} In the summer, I average about 200 miles a week on my sleek carbon steed. I do like pasta before a big ride. But many times I like the protein power and the lightness of turkey to help repair my sore muscles.

This will help fuel a hike, a ride, a run or a walk. Light yet creamy. And it packs a little kick with the addition of crushed red pepper. Perfecto to supercharge your next adventure.

Ingredients

½ pound vegetable radiatore, or other short cut pasta
1 tablespoon olive oil
½ medium onion, diced
sea salt & black pepper. freshly ground - to taste
crushed red pepper, to taste
½ lb ground turkey (I used dark meat)
2 cloves garlic, minced
¼ cup white wine
¼ cup chicken stock
3 cups fresh spinach
¼ teaspoon nutmeg
1 cup Parmesan cheese, grated + more for garnish
¼ cup half & half

Preparation

Let's set the mood, shall we? Drop and give me 10 pushups or crunches. Trust me, you'll like this. (Even though you thought I would send you straight for the wine...)

OK, are you done?

Feel the endorphin rush of exercise. It will help you stay young Mon Cheri.

Now let's cook.

- Bring salted water to a boil in your large pot for the pasta.
- Coat a 12 inch skillet with olive oil over medium heat. Now add onion, red pepper flakes salt, and pepper. Cook 6-8 minutes or until onion is tender and begins to caramelize lightly, stirring occasionally.
- Cook the pasta and cook al dente. Drain and set aside, reserving ¼ cup of the pasta cooking liquid.
- Add garlic to your skillet and stir continuously for another minute. Now introduce the turkey and cook until brown, stirring from time to time.
- Add the wine and the chicken stock. Mix in well and allow to boil and reduce for 4-5 minutes.
- Turn the heat to low and put in your lovely spinach, tossing it gently until it begins to wilt. Add the nutmeg (freshly grated is way more amazing!) Add ½ of your reserved pasta cooking water and the half & half. Adjust the consistency with more pasta water if you wish. Stir well and remove from the heat.
- Pile the pasta into a family style bowl and spoon the turkey/sauce mixture on top. Add heaps of Parmesan.

Tomorrow you will effortlessly accelerate at will.

FREE BONUS: The Smashed Chef's Unique and Intuitive Wine Pairing Guide, Filled with Gourmet Tips & Tricks. *www.lovesharecook.com/smashed-chef.*

77

TANKED-UP BOILED PASTA

COOK TIME: 15 MINUTES

Pasta, cooked in wine. Now that's-a-Italian!

This dish is perfect for leftover rotisserie chicken. You could also use pre-cooked chicken pieces you can find in the deli aisle in the super-market, right by the pre-cut and packaged meats (if your grocer is wise...) Heck, you could just buy a whole rotisserie chicken and use the rest for one of the earlier soup recipes! The point is, it's going to save you a lot of time. Time you don't have to spend cooking tonight.

In 15 mere minutes, you will create a taste sensation that will impress your friends, your family and even that special someone over candle light.

This pasta is seriously tanked up. It takes on an intense flavor, while chicken adds protein to this very fresh tasting dish. Then, the cheese takes it over the top. Here's to preparing a luxurious meal, in 15 minutes.

I show you how, YOU collect the praise. You're a miracle worker.

Ingredients

1 Box fettuccine
Leftover rotisserie chicken meat cut in chunks
2 tablespoon. olive oil divided
fruity table wine
minced garlic
fresh lemon juice and zest
dash crushed red pepper
parmesan
mozzarella

Preparation

If the pasta is about to get a drink, a small sip of the wine is in order. You don't want to cook it in inferior wine, it must be drinkable too. Just a sip, this dish will be prepared at warp speed.

- Heat the wine to a rolling boil in a large pot. Add the fettuccine and cook until al dente. Drain the pot, and don't cry over spilt wine. Set aside.

- Now get out a 12 inch skillet and put it over medium heat with a tablespoon of olive oil. Add the chicken and a dash of crushed red pepper.

- Add the other tablespoon of oil to the pan and add the pasta. Add the lemon zest and fresh lemon juice and mix.

- Put in bowls and be as generous as you like with the parmesan and the mozzarella.

- Bask in the praise of a dish that only took a quarter of an hour.

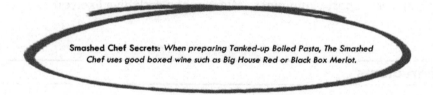

Smashed Chef Secrets: *When preparing Tanked-up Boiled Pasta, The Smashed Chef uses good boxed wine such as Big House Red or Black Box Merlot.*

FREE BONUS: The Smashed Chef's Unique and Intuitive Wine Pairing Guide, Filled with Gourmet Tips & Tricks. *www.lovesharecook.com/smashed-chef.*

79

BOMBED BAKED ZITI

COOK TIME: 1:25

Bombed and Baked. That's how I describe my party boy rocker client. This one's for you Johnny.

Now, it's time for you to be a rocker. Tis' time to get your ziti bombed before it gets baked (legally, unlike Johnny...) That's it; get your diva attitude on. Turn on some Pat Benatar.

I'm being a bad boy, giving you another dish that takes longer than 40 minutes. Bad me. I'm a rebel. But the prep time is short, about 15-20 minutes. More time for you to sing and dance. Perfect for a lazy Sunday.

And of course you and all your rocker pals will thank me for this sinfully good baked pasta. This dish has great chew, a rich, cheesy baked dish of pasta yumminess. Worthy of a rock diva like you.

Ingredients

1 (16 oz.) box baked ziti
1 lb. chopped beef or pork
1 med. onion, chopped
16 oz. Ricotta cheese
1 lg. pkg. Mozzarella
1 egg
½ c. red wine
1 teaspoon. oregano
½ teaspoon. garlic powder
16 oz. jar spaghetti sauce
1 c. sliced mushrooms

Preparation

- Strut to the kitchen and put a big pot on the stove with salted water and bring to a boil.
- Cook your ziti according to Preparation, staying on the fast side of the suggested time so it comes out al dente.
- In a 12 inch skillet, sauté the chopped meat and onion until meat is browned on all sides. Drain out the fat. Mix your ziti into the meat/onion mixture.
- Now, in a separate bowl grab your egg, crack it and beat it. Beat it good. Mix in the oregano and garlic powder. Now add the ricotta the jar of the spaghetti sauce and the wine. Mix well.
- Mix the meat and onion mixture thoroughly with the pasta, and then add the ricotta sauce mixture. Put it in an oven safe pan and top with thick slices of mozzarella. Bake for an hour at 350.
- Let it set for 5 minutes and plate up. *Bon Appétit* my diva friend.

BAKED PASTA SHELLS FILLED WITH CROCKED FENNEL YUMMINESS

COOK TIME: 40 MINUTES

When it's cold outside, and you crave pasta, a baked pasta dish satisfies. Here in Idaho, our winters are long and the snow can pile up so much you don't want to leave home. This is one of my favorite dishes when I'm socked in... and have fennel awaiting me in the crisper.

Fennel has a crunchy texture, slightly sweet and has a licorice like flavor. It makes for a refreshing Mediterranean style dish. The bulb, stalks, leaves and even the seeds are edible.

In Italy, you can find fantastic fennel at any street market when it's in season. At a good grocer you can get it almost year around. Braising the fennel with carrots and onion brings out the best in all of them.

Add that to pasta... bake it with a parmesan crust and create a cozy warm home that's perfect for snuggling.

Ingredients

32 (or more, it's 8 each) giant pasta shells or *conchiglioni*
6 small fennel bulbs
1 large onion
1 large carrot
1 sprig of rosemary, the leaves only
1-1½ glass of dry white wine
parmesan, freshly grated
salt
extra-virgin olive oil

Preparation

- Start a pot of salted water to boil. Pour a glass of wine to warm yourself. Pre-heat your oven to 400.

- Now slice the fennel, onion and carrot and sauté them slowly in a 12 inch pan on medium low in olive oil. Salt to taste.

- After about 2-3 minutes add your wine and the rosemary and go on braising until the liquid is gone and vegetables are soft and slightly golden.

- Run the vegetables in a food processor or blender until creamy. There may be small chunks, that's perfectly fine.

- Add a little olive oil to your water and add the pasta. The oil will make it easier to separate the shells when done. Cook al dente and remove from water and separate on a fairly deep greased cookie sheet or form.

- Now fill the pasta shells with fennel mixture using a spoon. Fill them nice and full. Top with a generous amount of parmesan cheese and add water to cover bottom. Carefully place in your pre-heated oven for 20 minutes, or until lightly browned on top.

- Plate them up, 2 to a plate for 4 servings. Or you may want more. It's up to you on this cold night where snuggling is in order.

FREE BONUS: The Smashed Chef's Unique and Intuitive Wine Pairing Guide, Filled with Gourmet Tips & Tricks. *www.lovesharecook.com/smashed-chef.*

83

ORZO AND WINO

COOK TIME: 15 MINUTES

Orzo is different. Just like you. It's a refreshing break from your same old-same old pastas and has a texture all of its own and looks like rice. You can find it in most markets as it's an ingredient for rice pilafs.

I always have orzo in my pantry, as it is usually well stocked. However, there are some times when I have depleted it. Yes, I'm busy just like you are. I cook for my lady, but I also write, ride my bicycle, and ski. So when I'm focused on my other passions, I may procrastinate about going to the store.

A few years ago, my pantry was in such a pickle. Shelves were bare and I had to pack that night for a private chef gig in Beverly Hills. I had friends coming over for a farewell dinner, and no time to go to the store.

But necessity is sometimes the mother of invention. Even though the cupboards were nearly bare, there are a few things The Smashed Chef ALWAYS has. Orzo, butter, wine and parmesan!

Those simple ingredients are enough to create a feast. Out of thin air, I created a textural masterpiece. A tangy blend of the orzo and wine with a buttery finish. Perfection with few ingredients. This is what makes cooking fun. The dish was so well received, I've created it many times since. Even when the pantry is fully stocked.

Ingredients

1 lb orzo pasta
6 tablespoons salted butter
½ teaspoon salt
½ teaspoon pepper
½ cup white wine
½ cup parmesan cheese

Preparation

It's time to get creative with a VERY limited ingredient list. For tonight you are in a rush... and it's time to get cooking.

- Fill a pot with salted water and boil. Add the pasta and cook as directed.
- Strain the orzo and return it to your pot.
- Add dry white wine and butter. Cook down for 1-3 minutes while constantly stirring
- Salt and pepper to taste and grate fresh Parmesan cheese on top.
- Now go pack for that business trip.

85

GODDESS HAIR WITH SMOKED SALMON AND DILL

COOK TIME: 20 MINUTES

Back to capellini... angel hair pasta, or as I call it – Goddess Hair. Tonight we shall create a meal fit for a goddess. A salty, savory brine of goodness served over pasta.

I love the flavor of dill and salmon. I remember the first time I tasted that combination in the Pacific Northwest, visiting grandparents on Mercer Island, near Seattle. At the time, my palate was decidedly European. I was 13 and had never been to the U.S., although I was raised as an American.

My grandfather was rather well-to-do and he enjoyed fishing on his boat. He also enjoyed smoking his own fish. On that trip I experienced both for the first time. And my grandmother made a dish similar to this the night before my mother and I returned to northern Italy.

The pasta was made delightful with the addition of the sharp flavor of dill with the salty smoky salmon and capers. The creamy, fresh tasting sauce begged to be blotted up with bread.

This is a dish for 2. Of course you may double it, but aren't you due for some romance this night?

Ingredients

6 ounces angel hair pasta
½ cup whipping cream
½ cup whole milk (do not use low-fat or nonfat)
¼ cup chopped fresh dill
¼ cup chopped green onions
1½ tablespoons drained capers
1 teaspoon grated lemon peel
4 ounces thinly sliced smoked salmon, cut into thin strips

Preparation

Set the mood tonight. Dim the lights and add beautiful music. Feel the love and get ready to add it to your cooking... Yes, a glass of wine couldn't hurt. Let's have some fun and cook.

- Start a large pot of salted water and bring it to a boil. Cook the pasta until al dente. Drain the pasta and return it to your pot.
- Now gently combine the cream, milk, dill, onions, capers and lemon peel in heavy saucepan over medium-high heat. Bring everything to a boil.
- After the mixture has boiled a minute or two, pour over the pasta and toss to coat it completely .
- Finally, add your smoked salmon and toss to combine everything, but not too much as to pulverize the salmon. Season with salt and pepper to taste.
- Put the pasta mixture into 2 shallow bowls. You just put more love in a bowl. Your love is endless.

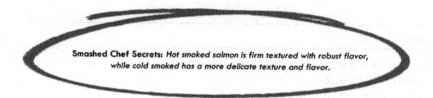

Smashed Chef Secrets: *Hot smoked salmon is firm textured with robust flavor, while cold smoked has a more delicate texture and flavor.*

FREE BONUS: The Smashed Chef's Unique and Intuitive Wine Pairing Guide, Filled with Gourmet Tips & Tricks. *www.lovesharecook.com/smashed-chef.*

87

SLOSHED SPINACH AND CHEESE STUFFED PASTA SHELLS

COOK TIME: 40 MINUTES

Sometimes it's good to go meatless. On those occasions, cheesy stuffed pasta shells are just the ticket. Here is a decedent vegetarian main course for such occasions.

This is a variation of a dish I use for large banquets. It is good to have a variety of foods available. You never know if there's a vegetarian in the crowd... and hey, they need sustenance too.

I've made this quicker by using frozen spinach and marinara in a jar. Otherwise, it's the exact same. Still delicious. The fennel seeds add a unique flavor your meatless friends will long for again and again. Go ahead, share the recipe with them.

Ingredients

2 10-ounce packages frozen chopped spinach, thawed
15 ounces ricotta cheese
1 cup (about 4 ounces) grated Parmesan
2 tablespoons fennel seeds
2 tablespoons chopped fresh basil or 2 teaspoons dried, crumbled
3 garlic cloves, minced
Salt and pepper
3½ cups prepared marinara or spaghetti sauce
32 jumbo pasta shells, freshly cooked
Additional grated Parmesan

Preparation

- Preheat oven to 350.

- Start a pot of salted water to boil. When boiling, add a little olive oil to your water and cook the pasta. Cook al dente and remove from water. Separate on a lightly olive oiled cookie sheet and set aside.

- Gently dry spinach on paper towels, squeezing out excess moisture. Put dried off spinach in a large bowl. Add the ricotta cheese, ½ cup Parmesan, basil, fennel and minced garlic to the bowl. Season to taste with salt and pepper, and mix.

- Spoon a ½ cup of your marinara sauce evenly over bottom of large baking dish. Fill each pasta shell with the spinach/cheese mixture using a spoon. Put the shells, filling side up, in your baking dish. Spoon all of the remaining sauce over the shells. Dust the tops with your remaining ½ cup of Parmesan.

- Cover with a loose foil tent and bake approximately 25 minutes. Serve in the cooking dish. After plating, cover with fresh Parmesan to taste.

You're amazing. You can cook vegetarian ;-)

FREE BONUS: The Smashed Chef's Unique and Intuitive Wine Pairing Guide, Filled with Gourmet Tips & Tricks. *www.lovesharecook.com/smashed-chef.*

89

FUNKY FENNEL AND SAUSAGE RAGU WITH PASTA

COOK TIME: 35 MIN

I had to add another great fennel recipe to this amazing pasta collection. It's a truly Italian ingredient, perfect for a rustic farm style dish. Not to mention I have found very few women who don't enjoy the flavor. At least when it's prepared correctly.

I love adding fennel to a thick, sausage ragù, or thick meat sauce for pasta. If I had a favorite ragù, this would be it. I learned it from a dear friend who has a farm in Italy, and modified it slightly to make it fast.

After all, you're hungry and in a rush. What is it tonight, yoga class? Nasty boss sent you home with more work? Behind on the laundry? Let's save you some time in the kitchen tonight and prove you truly are an amazing super-multi-tasking gourmet.

Ingredients

1 fennel bulb with fronds (leaves)
1 medium onion, chopped
1 tablespoon olive oil
1 lb sweet Italian sausage (bulk)
½ cup dry white wine
2 cups prepared marinara sauce
1 lb rotini, fusilli, or other spiral pasta

Preparation

- Bring a large pot of salted water to a boil.
- Trim off the fennel stems from the bulb. Chop and reserve 2 tablespoons of the leaves and chop up the bulb.
- In a 12-inch heavy skillet, over medium high, sauté the fennel bulb and onion in olive oil, stirring just until it begins to brown. Add the sausage and brown while stirring and breaking meat up into bite sized pieces.

90

- After all of the pink is gone, add the wine and simmer until reduced by about half, 7-8 minutes. Add the marinara sauce and simmer, stirring often, until vegetables are tender and sauce thickens for approximately 10 more minutes.
- While sauce simmers, cook pasta until al dente, 8 minutes. Drain, toss and finish 2 minutes in sauce. Garnish with fennel fronds.
- Now that's-a-Italiano! The rest of your to-do list doesn't stand a chance with this rocket fuel...

RAPID RAVIOLI with CREAMED TOMATO SAUCE

COOK TIME: 16 MINUTES

It's funny, most of my vegetarian friends love wine. Organic, of course. When I have them over for dinner they repeatedly raid my small wine cellar and taunt me for my carnivorous eating habits.

The last time I made this dish for a vegetarian couple who loved all things ravioli and wine, I had just bought a half case of an amazing organic Pinot Noir from Oregon. It went perfect with this hearty dish.

This is the perfect dish to prepare at the end of the tomato growing season, when they are at the peak of flavor. It's a creamy, luxurious sauce that begs to be soaked up with bread. And by using pre-packaged ravioli, it only takes 16 minutes. (Including seeding and chopping tomatoes!)

Just don't let your friends find your secret organic wine stash. If they are like mine... it will soon be gone. Trust me, your Pinot stash is AT RISK. You have been warned.

Ingredients

9 oz. purchased 4-cheese ravioli
3 tablespoons extra-virgin olive oil
6 garlic cloves, minced
2 pounds ripe tomatoes, seeded and chopped
1 cup dry white wine
$1/3$ cup whipping cream
2 tablespoons chopped fresh tarragon
½ cup grated Parmesan cheese

Preparation

- Heat a large pot of salted water until gently boiling. Fresh ravioli need gentle care. Turn off burner and cook pasta according to Preparation. It should only take about 4 minutes. Drain, separate and set aside.

- Heat oil over medium-high heat in a heavy 12 inch skillet. Add garlic and sauté for about 30-45 seconds. Add the seeded, chopped tomatoes and simmer them for about 5 minutes.

- Stir in the wine and simmer for 3-4 more minutes. Mix in the cream and tarragon and simmer until lightly thickened, about 2 more minutes.

- Grate in cheese and stir. Season with salt and pepper to taste.

- Place ravioli in bowls and ladle sauce over the top. Serve with more cheese of course.

- And make sure you don't put ALL of your Organic Pinot where your friends can find it.

FREE BONUS: The Smashed Chef's Unique and Intuitive Wine Pairing Guide, Filled with Gourmet Tips & Tricks. *www.lovesharecook.com/smashed-chef.*

93

PLASTERED PASTA FAGIOLI

COOK TIME: 40 MINUTES

Even though much of our food and lifestyle were Italian, my home was decidedly American. My father insisted I grow up that way. Friends would send VCR tapes of American TV. We still made hamburgers and ate apple pie from time to time to remind us who we were.

So I was a curiosity in the small towns of Italy.

Now any good cook in Italy has an arsenal of different pasta recipes. Usually these recipes are handed down generation after generation. As a cooking curious young man, I had a unique opportunity to weasel my way into homes of the locals. After all, I was the "American" and I was different.

My favorite home to raid for cooking lessons was the home of the Bianchi's. Signora Bianchi was a small lady with a big heart. She was loved by everyone in town, and she had mastered Pasta Fagioli... a delicious and rustic meatless dish with beans.

I modeled Signora Bianchi's dish for you. In less than one tenth the time.

Ingredients

2 slices of bacon, chopped
1 small onion, chopped fine
1 garlic clove, minced
1 small rib of celery, chopped fine
1 carrot, sliced thin
1½ cups chicken broth
16-ounce can white beans, rinsed well and drained
16-ounce can tomatoes, drained and chopped
$^1/_3$ cup tubetti or other small tubular pasta
2 tablespoons minced fresh parsley leaves
freshly grated Parmesan as an accompaniment

Preparation

- Use a heavy saucepan and cook the bacon over medium heat. Stir frequently until it is crisp. Pour off all but 1 tablespoon of the bacon fat, and sauté the onion and garlic for 3-4 minutes, stirring occasionally until the onion is softened.

- Now add the celery, carrot and broth. Cover and simmer the mixture for about 5 minutes.

- In a separate bowl, mash ⅓ cup of the beans. Stir them into the bacon mixture with the rest of the beans and your tomatoes. Gently simmer, covered, stirring sporadically, for about 5 minutes.

- Add the tubetti, stir, cover and simmer for 10 minutes, or until the pasta is al dente. If it gets too thick, add a touch more wine like Signora Bianchi always would.

- Take off heat and let soup sit covered for 5 more minutes to meld the flavors.

- Garnish with Italian flat leaf parsley and serve in bowls with Parmesan cheese grated on top and a loaf of Italian bread.

- Enjoy a century old recipe, updated to a quick dish that fits into your busy life.

FREE BONUS: The Smashed Chef's Unique and Intuitive Wine Pairing Guide, Filled with Gourmet Tips & Tricks. *www.lovesharecook.com/smashed-chef.*

95

SOUSED ITALIAN TUNA WITH SALSA CRUDA ON PASTA SHELLS

COOK TIME: 25 MINUTES

In Italy a no-cook pasta sauce is known as salsa cruda, and makes a wonderful one-dish dinner. It is very sensuous. This is a dish I often prepare when I arrive home from a client job out of town. Those are the evenings I wish to spend with my lover in other ways...

You deserve such romance. Your fuel shall be pasta, a bit of tuna for protein and a lush raw pasta sauce. Tonight you can create a special night of wine, pasta and passion. Yes, perhaps it is a weeknight, but there will never be another tonight Mon Cheri.

In this version, the combination of artichokes, olives, capers, and lemon zest is not only beautiful, but bold in flavor. Be daring tonight, it's an extraordinary moment in time to escape the drudgery of routine, and dance with your lover.

Ingredients

3 tablespoons salt
1 pound small pasta shells
Salsa Cruda:
1 (6-ounce) jar artichoke hearts, drained
¼ cup drained and rinsed capers
½ cup pitted and chopped Kalamata olives
juice and zest of 1 lemon
2 (6½ ounce) cans imported Italian tuna in olive oil, drained
½ cup extra-virgin olive oil
¼ cup dry white wine dry white wine
freshly ground black pepper to taste
½ cup chopped fresh flat-leaf parsley leaves

Preparation

Brace yourself. Pour a glass of wine and lose your inhibitions. You're about to make naked pasta sauce. How bold you are?

- In a 10-quart pot, bring the water to a brisk boil. Add salt and stir in the pasta shells. When the water returns to a boil, begin timing and cook al dente according to the package Preparation.

- Reserve ¼ cup of the pasta cooking water. Drain the pasta, but do not rinse. Transfer the shells to a large serving bowl. Stir in the reserved pasta water to keep the pasta from sticking to itself.

- Pasta continues to cook and absorb water even when it has been drained. Add in the salsa cruda ingredients and toss. Garnish with chopped parsley leaves.

- Light the candles. Sit next to your lover. Ask (with a wink) if he or she likes naked pasta sauce.

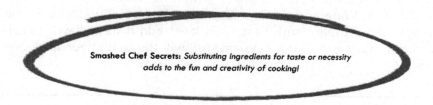

Smashed Chef Secrets: *Substituting ingredients for taste or necessity adds to the fun and creativity of cooking!*

FREE BONUS: The Smashed Chef's Unique and Intuitive Wine Pairing Guide, Filled with Gourmet Tips & Tricks. *www.lovesharecook.com/smashed-chef.*

97

SHRIMP AND LEEK LOADED LINGUINE

COOK TIME: 30 MINUTES

Many lovers fall into routines. I have always tried to avoid such boredom. Keeping it spicy makes life all the more delightful. Don't you agree?

It's as easy to fall into that trap in the kitchen as it is the bedroom. Not that tomato based or cream sauces are all that dull. But sometimes it's good to be unpredictable.

Tonight is a good night to show that flair of creativity and unpredictability. It will light the flames of love and show your lover a whole new side of you.

Your adventurous side will shine with this deliciously light pasta preparation. Wine and garlic create a lovely sauce. Succulent shrimp provide the protein. Fresh herbs and leeks add a fresh flavor that is far from routine. And the pepperoncini will showcase your spicy side tonight.

Ingredients

1 pound small uncooked shrimp, peeled, deveined, shells reserved
1 ¾ cups water
6 tablespoons olive oil
2 large garlic cloves, minced
2½ cups thinly sliced leeks (white and pale green parts only from about 2 large)
¼ cup thinly sliced stemmed drained pepperoncini (about 4 whole)
3 tablespoons chopped fresh oregano
2 teaspoons minced lemon peel
¼ cup dry white wine
2 tablespoons fresh lemon juice
1 pound linguine
Chopped fresh parsley

Preparation

- In a large pot, heat salted water to boil for the pasta.

- Now place the shrimp shells in a separate medium saucepan. Add 1 ¾ cups water and a liberal pinch or two of salt. Bring this to boil over medium-high heat. Cover, decrease heat to medium-low and simmer for 15 minutes until reduced to approximately 1 cup of shrimpy stock. Strain into measuring cup, pressing on shells with the flat side of a spoon to extract as much stock as you can.

- Meanwhile, heat 3 tablespoons of olive oil in a heavy 12 inch skillet over medium-high heat. Add the shrimp meat and sauté for 2 minutes until opaque. Transfer shrimp meat to a medium sized bowl.

- Reduce your heat to low. Add remaining 3 tablespoons of olive oil to that same skillet. Add the garlic and sauté for 1 minute until soft, but not too brown. Add the leeks, pepperoncini, oregano, and lemon peel. Cover and cook until the leeks soften, about 4 to 6 minutes.

- Now add the wine, lemon juice, and shrimp stock. Increase the heat to high and boil until reduced by half, about 3-4 minutes. Remove from heat.

- Cook pasta in until al dente, stirring occasionally so it doesn't stick. Drain and reserve 1 cup of the pasta cooking liquid.

- Add the pasta and shrimp to your skillet with the sauce and mix well to coat. Add reserved cooking liquid until you like the consistency. Season to taste with salt and pepper.

- Plate your pasta and pour any remaining sauce over each dish evenly. Garnish with Italian flat leaf parsley.

- Be unpredictable with your lover after dining. Wink at him while dining. Go for a romantic walk and hold her hand. Rekindle your connection.

Smashed Chef Secrets: Small changes in your kitchen can make cooking much more fun! A new high-end knife, a new stainless steel pasta pot, or even a nice garlic press brings you new toy options for the kitchen. With the money you save cooking yourself, you can afford it. Plus you deserve a shopping trip.

FREE BONUS: The Smashed Chef's Unique and Intuitive Wine Pairing Guide, Filled with Gourmet Tips & Tricks. *www.lovesharecook.com/smashed-chef.*

99

BLITZED BOW-TIE PASTA WITH ZUCCHINI

COOK TIME: 45 MINUTES

How amazing does your lover look when he dresses "Black Tie?" Handsome and debonair? I thought so. It is a stunning, classic look the Smashed Chef enjoys. With my lover on my arm at a gallery opening or a fundraiser, I feel on top of the world.

Food can be that elegant. That simple. That delicious.

On Black Tie evenings, I love simple fare. One evening my lady and I went to an art gallery opening of one of our favorite artists. Hors d'oeuvres were being served, along with new offerings from a local winery.

A busy work day had made us both ravenous. A light meal was just what we needed to take the edge off of our hunger. From our small garden that afternoon, I picked fresh zucchini and basil. I had no idea what I would create. But simplicity is always a good menu choice.

Combining the fresh flavor of basil added complexity to the neutral tasting zucchini. Butter and cheese add a savory element that's not too heavy. Bow Ties for Black Tie night. It has become a tradition.

Ingredients

6 small zucchini
2 teaspoons salt
2 cups packed fresh basil leaves
1 pound farfalle
¼ cup extra-virgin olive oil
¼ cup dry white wine
3 tablespoons unsalted butter
½ cup finely grated fresh Parmigiano-Reggiano plus additional for serving

Preparation

- Cut zucchini crosswise into 1/8 inch thick segments. Place zucchini in a colander, and generously salt them. Put paper towels between layers of zucchini slices. The salt and towels will take out the excess moisture. Let the zucchini set 45 minutes. Pat the zucchini dry.
- While zucchini is in the colander, bring a pasta pot with salted water to a boil. Cook pasta in boiling water until al dente. Drain pasta and reserve 1 cup of pasta cooking liquid. Cut your basil into thin strips, lengthwise.
- While pasta is cooking, heat oil over medium high in a deep 12-inch heavy skillet heat. Sauté the zucchini. Stir occasionally until golden and tender for approximately 7 minutes. Add the wine and cook 1 more minute.
- Now reduce heat to low and stir in half of your basil strips. Stir in cooked pasta and butter and lovingly toss until the butter is completely melted.
- Now, stir in half of your reserved pasta water and gently toss. Add more pasta water if too dry. Toss with ½ cup Parmigiano-Reggiano, and the rest of the basil. Salt and pepper to taste.
- Serve pasta with copious amounts of additional cheese.

Your dress for tonight is far too elegant to dine in. Put it on after eating. Allow your lover to zip the back. Make sure his tie is straight. Tonight is going to be a lovely evening of culture with the one you love.

PASTA PAELLA A LA SMASHEY

COOK TIME: 40 MINUTES

Three years ago, while on assignment in England, I read an interesting article on Mail Online (a UK based online news service) about the best lovers in the world. The Smashed Chef is interested in such things.

While the Swedes were bashed for being too quick, and the English for being too lazy, the world's best lovers were decidedly Spanish. In Spain, lovers are generous. Passionate. Spain is a country steeped in romantic culture.

Like a good lover, paella has passion. But it takes a long time to cook. You don't have that time tonight, so here's a great shortcut method with all of the flavors of paella sure to light the fires of passion in your home.

Substituting the rice with fideos, (Spanish dried coiled vermicelli noodles), cuts the cooking time dramatically while the seafood, chorizo and saffron add a Spanish flair that will show your lover how hot-blooded you are this evening. Not only can you climb the corporate ladder and still cook... you can cook.

Ingredients

1 medium zucchini
4 plum tomatoes
1 medium onion
2 garlic cloves
2 tablespoons olive oil
Dash of saffron
6 ounces fideos, or 6 ounces thin spaghetti broken into 2-inch pieces
¼ pound chorizo links or hot Italian sausage links
1¼ cups water
¾ cup dry white wine
12 small hard-shelled clams such as littlenecks (less than 2 inches in diameter)
12 medium sized shrimp, peeled
1 tablespoon chopped fresh parsley leaves

Preparation

This is the time to pour a fine glass of Riojas, one of the premier wines of Spain. Picture a romantic evening overlooking the sea and escape the stresses of this day. Laugh. It is time to cook something wondrous.

- Slice the zucchini and tomatoes into ½-inch pieces. Chop the onion and mince the garlic. Keep the vegetables separate.

- In a heavy Dutch oven, heat oil over medium high heat until shimmery. Quickly sauté the uncooked pasta, turning until golden for about 2 minutes.

- With a slotted spoon transfer pasta to a bowl. In the oil that remains in your Dutch oven, sauté the zucchini with a pinch of salt. Stir intermittently, until browned for about 3-4 minutes. Remove to another bowl.

- Now, chip up chorizo or squeeze sausage from casings into the Dutch oven and add the onion and garlic. Sauté the mixture until browned for about 5 minutes. (If you are using sausage, break it up into small chunks.)

- Add the tomatoes, wine, saffron and water. Bring to a boil. Add pasta and clams and boil, uncovered, stirring occasionally for 6 minutes. Add the peeled shrimp for 2 more minutes or until clams are opened and pasta is al dente. Dispose of any unopened clams.

- Stir in zucchini and parsley and cook until heated through.

In Spain, La Cena (dinner) is not served until after 9 PM. What could bring out your inner-Spaniard like a romantic late meal with your lover?

LINGUINE WITH CHICKEN AND SUN-DRIED YUMMINESS

COOK TIME: 30 MINUTES

Centuries ago, Italian peasants did not have the means to refrigerate or can fresh tomatoes. So they dried tomato halves on their terra cotta tiled roofs. Then, they could enjoy "pomodori secchi" or dried tomatoes throughout the winter until fresh tomatoes were again available.

What a gift to the modern woman. All of that stress of working during the day and then working all night keeping up your home require good nutrition. Sun dried tomatoes are packed with it. Plus the added benefit of intense flavor.

Tonight you deserve to provide your body with both. An evening meditation in the kitchen will erase your stress. It will be fun and relaxing. Dinner need not be a chore.

This amazing linguine with chicken and sun dried tomato sauce is rich and flavorful. The copious amounts of basil gives it a fresh flavor. And the presentation with the sliced chicken breast on top with even more basil will display your flair for cooking. Tonight, enjoy a quiet meal with your love.

Ingredients

¼ cup plus 1 tablespoon olive oil
3 tablespoons balsamic vinegar
1 large garlic clove, minced
½ teaspoon sugar
1 cup chopped red onion
½ cup chopped drained oil-packed sun-dried tomatoes
¾ cup sliced fresh basil
4 skinless boneless chicken breast halves
½ cup low-salt chicken broth
¼ cup dry red wine
1 9-ounce package fresh linguine, freshly cooked

104

Preparation

- In a large pot, heat salted water to boil for the pasta.
- Prepare the sauce ingredients. Whisk ¼ cup olive oil, wine, balsamic vinegar, garlic and sugar in a bowl to blend. Stir in onion, tomatoes and ¼ cup basil until coated well. Season dressing with salt and pepper.
- Cook pasta until al dente. Drain and set aside

- Heat the remaining 1 tablespoon oil over medium-high heat in a 12 inch heavy skillet. Season chicken thoroughly with salt and pepper. Add the chicken breast halves to the skillet. Sauté the chicken until brown, for about 3 minutes on each side. Add the broth, the sauce ingredient mixture and ¼ cup basil and bring to a boil.
- Reduce heat to medium-low. Simmer uncovered until chicken is cooked through, the sauce reduces, and the flavors marry, about 4 minutes. Remove the skillet from heat. Transfer chicken to a plastic cutting board and slice thin.
- Divide pasta on 4 plates. Top each with 1 sliced chicken breast half. Spoon the sauce over the top. Garnish each plate with the remaining ¼ cup basil.

Fresh, wasn't it? Now it's your turn.

BLT BOW TIE

COOK TIME: 30 MINUTES

One of the things that makes cooking so fun is how you can transform your favorite flavors into completely new dishes. One warm summers afternoon while at my friends lake cabin on beautiful Lake Coeur d' Alene, he mentioned how good a BLT sounded. He dared me to create a BLT inspired dish. While I know he was "working" me to prepare dinner for him and our ladies... I quickly accepted.

With stakes attached of course...

A bottle of my favorite Stag's Leap Petite Syrah wine if the ladies raved about my new creation.

Creativity comes when your back is to the wall. I saw bow tie pasta in the pantry. In his garden, the arugula was at its peak. And the refrigerator was stocked with a slab of applewood smoked bacon from our local artisan butcher.

The arugula replaces lettuce in this cleverly prepared pasta dish. It's got a fresh, yet sassy flavor with a hint of heat. Perfect to let the evening breeze of the lake cool you.

Ingredients

1 pound farfalle (bow tie pasta)
12 bacon slices, cut into 1-inch pieces
1 28-ounce can diced tomatoes, drained
¼ teaspoon dried crushed red pepper
3 cups arugula
1 cup sliced green onions
1 cup thinly sliced fresh basil leaves
¼ cup dry white wine
1 cup (packed) grated fresh Parmesan cheese

Preparation

Bet your lover a bottle of superb wine you can rock his world with pasta tonight. Make sure it's something special. Now you're ready to cook and enjoy the spoils of a wager.

- Cook the bow tie pasta in a large pot of boiling salted water until al dente. Drain and set aside.

- In a 12 inch heavy skillet over medium-high heat, cook the bacon until crisp.

- Remove bacon with slotted spoon to drain on paper towels. Pour off all but 3 tablespoons of bacon drippings from the skillet. Add the tomatoes and crushed red pepper. Sauté for about 2-3 minutes until tomatoes soften.

- To the skillet, add the arugula, onions, ½ cup basil, and crisped bacon. Sauté about 2 minutes until the arugula and basil lightly wilt. Stir in the wine and bring the mixture to a simmer.

- Add the cooked bow tie pasta to sauce and toss to coat. Mix in ¾ cup Parmesan cheese and the remaining ½ cup basil. Cook for about 2 minutes, finishing the pasta until cheese melts and coats it, tossing it often. Season to taste with salt and pepper.

- Serve with additional cheese tableside. After you bask in praise, collect your bottle of Stag's Leap Petite Syrah.

Smashed Chef Secrets: *Cooking pasta perfectly is easy. Test at the lowest package cooking time by carefully pulling out a piece of pasta, letting it cool for a few seconds and then biting into it or cutting and looking for a thin line of starch in the middle.*

FREE BONUS: The Smashed Chef's Unique and Intuitive Wine Pairing Guide, Filled with Gourmet Tips & Tricks. *www.lovesharecook.com/smashed-chef.*

107

FAB FETTUCCINE WITH ASPARAGUS, MORELS AND GOAT CHEESE

COOK TIME: 35 MINUTES

And now for something completely different. A most creative dish packed with flavor and a cornucopia of textures.

When I moved to Idaho, I discovered morels were plentiful. But not many people pick them because they are afraid of wild mushrooms.

Fortunately, I learned about picking mushrooms in Italy. There it is much more common for people in the country to understand Mycology (the study of mushrooms and other fungi).

After picking one day a few hours' drive from Coeur d' Alene, I found out my lover had never eaten a morel. Immediately I decided to create a new dish to introduce them to her. I combined the mushrooms with three of her favorite ingredients, goat cheese, fresh asparagus and of course pasta.

Tonight will show your amazing artistic flair in the kitchen. You will create a veritable showcase of innovative flavors and textures. This creamy, rustic fettuccini is truly heavenly.

Ingredients

½ cup minced shallot
2 tablespoons unsalted butter
½ cup dry white wine
½ cup chicken broth
½ pound fresh morels, wash well, pat dry, trim and slice crosswise (Morels are available
    seasonally at specialty produce markets and some supermarkets, if not available,
    reconstitute 1.5 ounces dried in 3 cups warm water)
½ cup heavy cream
6 ounces mild goat cheese such as Montrachet, crumbled (about 1 ½ cups)
¾ pound asparagus, trimmed, cut into ½-inch pieces, and cooked in boiling salted water for 2
    to 3 minutes, or until tender
¼ cup minced fresh chives
¾ pound fettuccine

Preparation

You heard it here first, creativity is enhanced by wine. Pour a glass and let's get cooking my busy lady...

- In a heavy 12 inch skillet over medium low heat, cook the shallot in butter, stirring until softened. Add the wine, and simmer until the wine is reduced by half, about 6 minutes.
- Now add the broth and the morels and simmer covered for about 10 minutes or until the morels are nice and tender.
- Add the cream and the goat cheese and cook the mixture over low heat, stirring, until the cheese is melted. Stir in the asparagus, the chives, and salt and pepper to taste. Keep the sauce warm.
- In a large pot of boiling salted water, cook the fettuccine until it is al dente. Drain and toss the pasta in the skillet with sauce to finish.
- Plate up and enjoy. How was heaven my angel?

FREE BONUS: The Smashed Chef's Unique and Intuitive Wine Pairing Guide, Filled with Gourmet Tips & Tricks. *www.lovesharecook.com/smashed-chef.*

109

WHISKEY CHICKEN STROGANOFF

COOK TIME: 35 MINUTES

I love all types of alcohol. Wine, beer, tequila, gin—whatever it is, I'll drink it. Still, I've imbibed enough over the years to recognize that even though each type makes you "drunk," the overall effect can be quite different depending on what you're focused on. Everyone has their crazy tequila story. Some of you may have even sworn off drinking tequila for that very reason. This is but one example of how different types of alcohol incur different effects.

Cue whiskey. It's one of my favorite drinks even ignoring its side-effects. It tastes like a hard day's work, perhaps in the old American West. The effect it has on my lovers, however, is far more interesting.

You see, I've found that whiskey makes women...frisky. It turns a lover into a sexual machine. That is, *if* they'll drink it.

Therein lies the problem. Most of the women I've met over the years detest whiskey. Thus, I try to include it in as many meals as possible. That way, I get the same effects out of my lover without her objecting to the taste. Try it yourself. I guarantee you'll be impressed.

This chicken stroganoff is designed to be lighter than the traditional beef stroganoff. I love beef stroganoff, but it leaves people feeling too heavy for any after-dinner activities. Hopefully this will keep your lover in a feisty mood, while still packing a bunch of flavor.

Ingredients

Kosher salt
12 ounces egg noodles
3 tablespoons unsalted butter
1 small onion, chopped
4 ounces white mushrooms, sliced (about 2 cups)
1¼ pounds skinless, boneless chicken thighs, cut into chunks
2 tablespoons all-purpose flour
1 teaspoon paprika, plus more for topping
Freshly ground pepper
1 cup fat-free low-sodium chicken or mushroom broth
1 tablespoon Worcestershire sauce
¼ cup whiskey
½ cup sour cream, plus more for topping
2 tablespoons chopped fresh parsley

Preparation

- Fire up the pasta pot with lightly salted water.
- Using a large skillet, melt two tablespoons of butter and cook onions for about 2 minutes. Add mushrooms and cook for an additional 2 minutes. Add the rest of the butter, flour, paprika, whiskey, and chicken. Cook on stovetop until chicken is brown. This should take about 3 minutes.
- Start the egg noodles and cook according to package until al dente. Drain and set aside.
- Now add broth and Worcestershire sauce to your skillet and simmer until sauce thickens, about five minutes.
- Finally, stir in sour cream and adjust spices. Cook 3 more minutes to heat sour cream through.
- Spoon sauce over noodles on plates and scarf. Good luck tonight.

FREE BONUS: The Smashed Chef's Unique and Intuitive Wine Pairing Guide, Filled with Gourmet Tips & Tricks. *www.lovesharecook.com/smashed-chef.*

lll

EASY HAM AND CHEESE SOUFFLÉ

COOK TIME: 39 MINUTES

This dish is easy. Why? Because sometimes you need something that you can cook naked, incredibly drunk, and extremely preoccupied by your "house guest."

"But Smashed Chef, why not just prepare a grilled cheese or a frozen burrito like the rest of us?" you might ask.

It's simple really: because I'm a goddamn gourmet chef. Also, I've never charmed a single person with my skill at turning on a microwave and heating up the perfect frozen burrito. There's already a book for you if that's what you're looking for. I think it's called *Microwave Cooking for One*.

No, we make real food here. Food that will make you the center of attention, even when you're wasted and don't really understand the difference between cinnamon and cayenne pepper anymore. Luckily, this soufflé is simple enough that you could probably prepare it blacked out, though I don't recommend it.

You're an adult. Eat like one.

Ingredients

2 russet potatoes, peeled and cut into ½-inch cubes
Kosher salt
6 large eggs, at room temperature, separated
8 ounces Manchego or aged Provolone cheese, grated (2 cups)
1 tablespoon all-purpose flour
Freshly ground pepper
4 tablespoons extra virgin olive oil, plus more if needed
1 onion, thinly sliced
2 Anaheim chili peppers, seeded and thinly sliced
¼ pound boiled ham, cut into small cubes
1 teaspoon paprika
2 tablespoons chopped fresh parsley
1 clove garlic, minced
¼ cup sherry

Preparation

Alright, I sort of lied. Practice making this soufflé without drinking first, so you can get it down. This is one of those party tricks you practice a thousand times before you do it drunk. It's not like the party trick where you say, "Hey, I bet I could jump over that car," and then fail miserably.

- Separate the egg whites from yolks into two large mixing bowls. Stir the flour, cheese and pepper into the bowl containing the yolks and set aside.

- Pre-heat your oven to 400 F. In a pot of salted water, take cubed potatoes and boil covered 2 minutes or until tender. Drain off water.

- Using a 10 inch non-stick skillet on high, add the onions with olive oil and chilies. Add sherry and cook for 4 more minutes. Add the ham to the skillet and cook for an additional 3 minutes, stirring regularly. Put this mixture into a third bowl and set aside. Now, add 2 tablespoons of oil plus the cooked potatoes to the skillet. Allow them to brown for 4 minutes.

- Next, add garlic, parsley and paprika to potatoes and cook an additional minute. Then add the potatoes to the bowl with the other cooked ingredients.

- In a separate mixing bowl, beat egg whites with 2 tablespoons water and ½ teaspoon salt until soft peaks are formed. Mix a third of the whites with the yolk mixture and very gently fold the rest of the egg whites in. The more gentle the fold, the fluffier the soufflé.
- Make sure skillet is oiled and on a medium low heat. Cook the egg mixture covered for about 6 minutes until the top sets.
- Add the potato filling on top of the set up egg mixture still in the skillet and cook in the oven, uncovered, until eggs are set—about 5-7 minutes.
- Carefully remove from oven, cut and serve with a salad and pair with Pinot Grigio or Riesling. Bask in the glory of your creation.

SLOSHY SHERRY SALMON

COOK TIME: 40 MINUTES

"If you're going to work for me, you're gonna have to come out fishing at least once. Fresh Washington salmon? You *are* a chef, right? You can't pass up that opportunity."

My client, who we'll call "Tim," was right. Living in the Pacific Northwest, I was no stranger to relatively fresh salmon. Regardless, the idea of catching my own fish was appealing.

A few weeks later I awoke to Tim trying to break down the door of the carriage house I was staying in, or—as he called it—knocking. I fumbled about in the dark, trying to get my bearings. "Oh good, you're up," Tim said when I opened the door. Cheeky.

We rode out into the frigid coastal waters searching for Coho (silver) salmon. While Tim fumbled with his BlackBerry, inking the terms of yet another financial deal, I set about landing dinner. Like some sort of primitive hunter (though one equipped with the finest fishing equipment money can buy), I landed fish after fish in the boat. I was an angel of death, wreaking havoc on these poor salmon. I was judge, jury, and executioner. I was alive.

Few times in my life have I felt more completely alive than when I ate the fruit of my labors that night. I mean, come on. I turned a living thing into a dinner (this exact recipe, actually) with my *own hands*. It was like giving birth. Except I killed an animal. You know what I mean.

Ingredients

½ cup walnuts
Pinch of cayenne pepper
1 tablespoon fresh lemon juice
1 teaspoon honey
2 tablespoons diced roasted red pepper
1 tablespoon walnut oil
2 tablespoons extra virgin olive oil
¼ cup chopped fresh parsley
Kosher salt and freshly ground black pepper
2 tablespoons chopped fresh chives
1 teaspoon grated lemon zest
1 2 to 3-pound fillet of wild salmon (about 1 ½ inches thick)
⅓ cup dry sherry

Preparation

White wine or red tonight? It's up to you. I like both with salmon, a nice Chardonnay or a Pinot Noir will do. Pour yourself a glass.

- Soak your salmon fillets in sherry for ten minutes. Go ahead, it will enjoy the flavor. Pre-heat your oven to 350 F. Put walnuts on a cookie sheet and bake in oven until toasted nicely, about 7 minutes. Cool. Chop them finely and put them in a bowl. Now, to the walnuts add cayenne pepper, honey, lemon juice, roasted red pepper and walnut oil. Put in 1 tablespoon of olive oil and 2 tablespoons parsley along with ½ teaspoon salt and pinch of pepper.
- Set your oven to 425 F and remove salmon from sherry. Make an herb mixture with a tablespoon of olive oil, 2 tablespoons of parsley, lemon zest, chives, a half teaspoon salt and a dash of black pepper.
- Now rub this mixture into the salmon. Roast salmon with the skin side down in a baking dish until cooked. This should take about 13 minutes. The salmon worked hard for you in the oven, so let it rest a few minutes before dining. Serve with the walnut mixture on top.
- You needn't be afraid to cook (or catch) fish. You will never fear it again.

SHERRY BABY MEATLOAVES

COOK TIME: 40 MINUTES

I like cooking for kids. You know why? Because they're easy. *As long as they aren't your kids.*

Let me explain. When you're a parent, you're always concerned about your kids' nutritional needs. You force them to eat all sorts of stuff in the hopes that they'll grow up to be Bobby Joe, All-American football star. Broccoli, Brussels sprouts, cauliflower—hey, I love these things as an adult, but I'm not blaming kids for disliking them. After all, two of the three things on that list look like brains on top.

When my sister said my niece and nephew would be visiting and that they were "picky eaters," I laughed. Then I whipped up this meatloaf recipe. The secret? Absolutely slathered in a good old-fashioned ketchup glaze. Guess who didn't hear any complaints all night about the food?

When you want to splurge, or you just want to shut your kids up, think about trying out this recipe. It's delicious, the added sherry makes it nice and juicy, and the mixed meats prevent it from tasting flat. This meatloaf recipe would make a 1950's housewife proud.

If you're looking for a more gourmet take on meatloaf, keep on reading. There's one later on in the book.

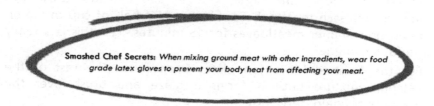

Smashed Chef Secrets: *When mixing ground meat with other ingredients, wear food grade latex gloves to prevent your body heat from affecting your meat.*

Ingredients

⅓ cup breadcrumbs
⅓ cup chopped fresh parsley
1 large egg
3 tablespoons Worcestershire sauce
1 small onion, finely minced
1 teaspoon chili powder
2 cloves garlic, grated or finely minced
1½ pounds meatloaf mix (ground beef, pork and/or veal)
Kosher salt and freshly ground pepper
1 tablespoon vegetable oil
⅓ cup sherry
½ cup ketchup
1 to 2 tablespoons packed light brown sugar
1 tablespoon apple cider vinegar

Preparation

If there are children about, a drink is in order. At least it always is for me. Your favorite wine will work wonders. Go ahead, I won't tell.

- Take the sherry, bread crumbs, egg, parsley, onion, chili powder and Worcestershire sauce and mix them in a large bowl. Add the meat, and salt and pepper to your liking. Mix well until everything is evenly incorporated into the meat

- Shape the mixture by hand, into approximately six evenly-sized loaves. Take a large skillet and heat vegetable oil on high. Brown the loaves in the skillet.

- In separate bowl, mix sugar, vinegar and ketchup. Brush this mixture on each meatloaf. To skillet, add a half of cup of water, cover and simmer meatloaves for 15 minutes. Yes, this is a really useful technique!

- Put the finished loaves on plate. Cook down the rest of the ketchup mixture until it forms a glaze and brush over the meatloaves again. Serve hot.

UNFLIPPING BELIEVABLE PORK WITH FENNEL SEED

COOK TIME: 40 MINUTES

I get to work with a lot of rock stars for one simple reason: I put alcohol in their food. Seriously, what kind of self-respecting musician could pass that deal up? On the other hand, most of my clients need a little convincing when it comes to trying new foods. Since I'm all about new foods, sometimes this leads to an argument.

Thus, it was with trepidation that I served this dish to my rock star client, "Dave." The scene: Dave's Las Vegas loft, replete with gorgeous women, expensive instruments, and "medicine," if you know what I mean. Dave woke up around four in the afternoon, cradling a beer and taking a hit of what he termed an "appetite stimulator."

Around five, it was breakfast time. I brought in a big plate of this pork recipe, hoping that the fennel would go over well. If you've read any of my other books, you know I love fennel almost as much as I love alcohol. I left him in peace with his plate full of pork.

Three minutes later I heard his voice resounding through the house, in a classic *I'm a rockstar and I get what I like* voice:

"This is flipping god DAMN unFLIPPING believable!"

Of course, what he actually said is unfit for print. I trust you get the idea. Any pork that can convince a hungover man to yell is good in my book, though.

Ingredients

4 1-inchthick boneless pork loin chops, sliced into ¼-inch strips
Salt and freshly ground black pepper
1 teaspoon fennel seed or ground fennel or fennel pollen
1 teaspoon crushed red pepper flakes, optional
¼ cup all-purpose flour
¼ cup white wine
4 tablespoons extra virgin olive oil
1 large fennel bulb, trimmed and thinly sliced, plus ¼ cup fennel fronds, chopped for garnish
1 onion, thinly sliced
3 to 4 garlic cloves, grated or finely chopped
2 tablespoons chopped fresh thyme leaves
3 tablespoons tomato paste
1 cup dry white or red wine
1 teaspoon orange or lemon zest, plus 2 tablespoons juice
1 cup chicken stock
¼ cup fresh flat-leaf parsley, chopped
1 loaf Ciabatta bread, cut into chunks and toasted, for serving

Preparation

Want to be a rock star? Start off cooking by taking a shot of your favorite libation. Otherwise, a glass of wine will suffice.

- Rub salt and pepper on the pork chops to season. Rub on the red pepper flakes and the fennel seed. You've added layers of flavor. Heat 3 tablespoons of olive oil on medium high in a 12-inch heavy skillet. Flour the pork chops and brown them over 5-6 minutes. Set pork aside.

- Add the remaining olive oil to the skillet and throw in sliced fennel bulb, garlic, thyme and onions. Cook until soft for about 8 minutes and then add the tomato paste, cooking for two more minutes. Add wine and mix with drippings. Put in juice, zest, stock and parsley.

- Lower the heat and let this mixture simmer an additional 5 minutes. Add the pork back into skillet and cook for 4 more minutes. Garnish the meat with chopped fronds of fennel. Serves up great with Ciabatta bread to sop up the juices. That's what rock stars do...

SWEET WHISKEY GLAZED CHICKEN

COOK TIME: 40 MINUTES

I've always been sort of obsessed with cowboys. Blame it on Sergio Leone. I was about to finish a contract working for a client in Palm Springs, CA when a friend asked me to go camping in Joshua Tree (right down the road). Desert country. Old West country.

I firmly believed that if I were to go camping in the Western US, there was only one method I could use. I accepted my friend's offer, but only if I could do it "proper." Not three-piece suit proper. Cowboy proper.

I went and bought a hat and some boots, put on a well-worn pair of jeans, and tucked in my plaid shirt. My friend shook his head at me, but I was determined to see this through. I stopped at a convenience store in Joshua Tree to pick up some last-minute touches: a can of beans and a bottle of whiskey.

The beginning of the night was spent uneventfully. I cooked my beans over an open fire like some sort of nineteenth century badass, washing it down with copious whiskey. It was after I passed out under the Joshua Tree stars that things got real.

Here's a hint for all readers: don't bother camping in the desert *during flash flood season*. I woke up as a huge wave of water hit me in the face and carried me downhill into our campsite. Oh, and did I mention I was covered in panicked ants because they got flooded out of their tunnels? To add insult to injury, I got a great sunburn the next day because our sunscreen washed away in the night. My only consolation was the small amount of whiskey left in my sand-encrusted bottle.

Damn you, Clint Eastwood. Damn you Sergio Leone.

FREE BONUS: The Smashed Chef's Unique and Intuitive Wine Pairing Guide, Filled with Gourmet Tips & Tricks. *www.lovesharecook.com/smashed-chef.*

121

Ingredients

2 tablespoons extra virgin olive oil
6 medium shallots
4 medium-large parsnips, peeled and cut into 1-inch chunks
$^1/_3$ cup apricot preserves
2 tablespoons whole-grain mustard
1 teaspoon ground ginger
½ teaspoon ground cumin
8 medium skin-on, bone-in chicken thighs
¼ cup whiskey
Kosher salt and freshly ground pepper
½ cup pitted prunes, roughly chopped
½ cup dried apricots, roughly chopped
1 tablespoon apple cider vinegar

Preparation

Come on, cowboy. Pour yourself a glass of whiskey and let's start cooking.

- Set your oven to 400° F and make sure to place the rack in the middle of the oven. Using a skillet that can be used in the oven, heat oil and add parsnips and shallots, cooking for 2 minutes.

- Mix whiskey, mustard, apricot preserves, ginger and cumin in a separate bowl to create a wonderful glaze.

- Use salt and pepper to rub on chicken pieces and toss the chicken with the apricot glaze. Next, put the dried fruit in the skillet and arrange the chicken thighs alongside the fruit with the skin side up. Add a quarter cup of water and boil. Cover the skillet and heat for 6 minutes on medium.

- Now, take the cover off and cook the chicken/vegetable mixture until the chicken is golden brown about 20 minutes. Move the contents of the skillet to one side and stir vinegar into the other side. This forms a sauce that is poured over chicken before serving.

- Place the cooked chicken, fruit and veggies in shallow bowls and pour the sauce over the top. Try not to get caught in a shootout.

DRUNK VINO VEAL CUTLETS

COOK TIME: 30 MINUTES

I love ships. Las Vegas tries to keep a monopoly on their "What happens in Vegas..." mentality, but let me tell you (as a seasoned partier), the really crazy stuff happens on ships.

It makes sense. 1) International waters. 2) Surrounded by people you will never, ever encounter in real life. 3) Everyone is drunk. 4) Cruise ship employees hate everyone onboard. Yes, even you.

But the best—*the BEST*—part of being onboard a ship? Built-in excuse to throw up, anytime and anywhere.

If I'm drunk and I have to get sick normally, it's awkward. Everyone feels sorry for that guy. If I'm drunk and get sick on a boat? "Seasickness." Who's going to get mad at me then? Only an asshole gets mad at the guy who's seasick. Don't be that asshole.

Oh yeah, I brought this up because this recipe uses Marsala. Marsala, like Port, is a wine fortified with extra alcohol so it could survive long ocean voyages in ye olden days. Some genius decided to keep the extra alcohol, even when we created an airplane that could cross the ocean in a matter of hours.

I wish I could shake the hand of that genius.

Ingredients

8 veal cutlets (about 3 ounces each)
Salt and freshly ground black pepper
2 to 3 tablespoons unsalted butter
2 to 4 tablespoons olive oil
1 large shallot, finely chopped
2 to 4 garlic cloves, smashed
2 ounces assorted mushrooms, sliced
½ cup sweet Marsala wine
¾ cup low-salt chicken broth
Leaves from 1 fresh rosemary sprig

FREE BONUS: The Smashed Chef's Unique and Intuitive Wine Pairing Guide, Filled with Gourmet Tips & Tricks. *www.lovesharecook.com/smashed-chef.*

123

Preparation

Tie a fake beard to your face, wear an eye patch, take a swig of Marsala, and get cooking.

- Rub salt and pepper onto veal pieces. In a large skillet, melt a tablespoon of butter and a tablespoon of oil over medium high heat. Cook cutlets until golden brown—about 1.5 minutes on each side.

- Remove the cutlets to a plate. Add another tablespoon of oil to your skillet, along with your garlic and shallots. Sauté for about 20 seconds. Add a tablespoon of oil for the mushrooms and sauté them for three minutes. Salt the mushrooms and add some of that precious Marsala wine.

- Simmer for 2 minutes and add the broth and leaves of rosemary. Simmer and reduce for another 4 minutes. Put the veal back in pot. Make sure all pan juices are added to the skillet, as well, and heat everything through for a minute.

- Add a tablespoon of butter to the mixture to thicken slightly and adjust the seasonings before serving.

- Enjoy with adventurous people, or at least pretend your house is a boat for the night. Blame everything on "seasickness."

LOADED SALSA GRILLED SALMON

COOK TIME: 23 MINUTES

"Again? Sure, I think we can make that work..." My client, Tim (who you might recall from our earlier Sloshy Sherry Salmon recipe) was looking at me a bit oddly. Perhaps he saw the blood-lust in my eyes. It had been a week since my first fishing trip, and I was thoroughly hooked. Pun most definitely intended.

This time around, I wasn't messing around. The first fishing trip I was but an unblooded novice. Now, I was a seasoned warrior. I even tried to grow a sailor beard to get further into the role, though I quickly abandoned it when I remembered how bad my beard-growing skills were.

When dawn came, I was already awake. Tim seemed surprised as I bounded out the door with no prompting, rod strapped across my back like a proper sword.

Still, there was something I had to clear up. "I saw this thing on the Internet...something about using dynamite to fish?"

"What?" said Tim. "No, we aren't doing that." He gave me another weird look. "Are you feeling okay?"

"Never better," I said, and got in the car.

Okay, so I didn't get to use dynamite, but I still caught enough fish to make this delicious meal for dinner: salmon topped with a fresh, fruity salsa. That's a pretty good consolation prize.

Ingredients

Salsa
2 large oranges
¼ cup extra virgin olive oil
¼ cup fresh lemon juice
¼ cup white wine
½ cup chopped fresh flat-leaf parsley
2 scallions, finely sliced
3 tablespoons chopped fresh mint leaves
2 tablespoons capers, rinsed, drained and coarsely chopped
2 tablespoons orange zest
1 teaspoon lemon zest
1 teaspoon crushed red pepper flakes
Kosher salt and freshly ground black pepper
Salmon
Vegetable or canola oil, for oiling the grill
4 (4- to 5-ounce) center cut salmon fillets, skinned, each about 3-inches square
2 tablespoons amber agave nectar
Kosher salt and freshly ground black pepper

Preparation

- For the salsa, take off the ends of the oranges, peel and free each segment. Cut them up into 2 or 3 pieces if you like smaller chunks. Put them in a bowl and add the lemon juice, white wine, parsley and olive oil. Throw in capers, mint, scallions, lemon and orange zest, and red pepper flakes. Add salt and pepper to taste.

- Set aside for the salmon.

- Brush the salmon with agave nectar, salt and pepper. Then grill salmon on an oiled grill or grill pan. Three to four minutes per side should do the trick for flaky salmon. When the salmon is cooked, serve immediately with salsa spooned over the top.

- A healthy, colorful dish in less than half an hour. What will you do with all of that extra time tonight? You don't have to tell me. I know the answer involves drinking, like a proper Smashed Chef student.

SAVORY SKIRT STEAK QUESADILLAS WITH FIXINGS

COOK TIME: 40 MINUTES

If you remember from earlier in our journey, I have a love-hate relationship with any place termed "wine country." On the one hand, it's normally easier to drink wine than water in these places. For the Smashed Chef, that certainly sounds like heaven. On the other hand, I have a tendency to "overdo" it (if such a thing is possible). Some people might say I "lose control."

First of all, those people are filthy liars. Second of all, those people are absolutely telling the truth. I can't contain myself when it comes to wine country. Thus, when a client in the software industry hired me to come stay at his second home in Washington's wine country, I accepted both wholeheartedly and yet with reservations. It was like an old cartoon, where the angel version of me was saying, "Don't do it! You'll screw it all up!" and the devil version was saying, "Wine."

Luckily (or unluckily, if you just like reading about me nearly dying all the time), my experience in Washington's wine country was a bit more tame than my past experiences in Sonoma County, California. Don't get me wrong: there were still parties, and way too many nights spent inebriated, but at least I didn't wake up in the wrong house.

Oh, and I came up with this delectable quesadilla recipe using my client's orchard, if you're into that sort of thing. Don't skip the apples: the texture they add is a big part of what makes this recipe work.

Ingredients

1 1-pound skirt steak
Salt and freshly ground black pepper
3 tablespoons vegetable oil
8 8-inch flour tortillas
2 cups shredded Mozzarella cheese, divided
¼ cup sherry
2 cups Roasted Tomatillo and Apple Salsa, recipe follows
Chunky Guacamole (recipe below)

Preparation

IMPORTANT: Make the Salsa and Guacamole while the meat tenderizes.

- Season the steak in a glass baking dish with salt and pepper rubbed in. Add sherry and let it tenderize for 15 minutes. Then, using a skillet and oil, cook steak until it is done, up to 10 minutes for well done. Let the meat rest away from heat for 5 minutes.

- Now slice thinly across the grain of the meat. Put two tortillas in skillet without cleaning it out. Sprinkle with half of the cheese, then half of the meat. Put 1 tortilla on top of each and cook each side two minutes. Repeat with remaining tortillas.

- When you remove the quesadillas from the skillet, peel them open and put a dollop of the Roasted Tomatillo and Apple Salsa inside. Cut quesadillas into quarter pieces. Serve alongside the Chunky Guacamole.

Roasted Tomatillo and Apple Salsa:

1 pound tomatillos, husked and rinsed
2 green apples, such as Granny Smith, quartered
2 whole cloves garlic, unpeeled
½ white onion
2 jalapeno chilies, stemmed
2 tablespoons olive oil
Salt and freshly ground black pepper

- Set oven to 350° F. Put the apples, garlic, tomatillos, onion and jalapenos on a cooking sheet. Toss these with olive oil, a teaspoon of pepper. Roast for 20 minutes. Peel the skin off of the garlic and puree this mixture until mostly smooth. Salt and pepper to taste.

Chunky Guacamole:

3 ripe avocados, cut into ½-inch dice
2 medium ripe tomatoes, seeded and cut into ½-inch dice
1 small white onion, finely chopped
¼ bunch fresh cilantro, chopped
½ Serrano chili, finely minced
2 small lemons, about 4 tablespoons
1 teaspoon kosher salt

- Put avocadoes, onion, tomatoes, Serrano chilies, lemon juice, cilantro and salt in a bowl. Stir and mash the avocado until well blended. Serve in a bowl alongside the quesadillas.

FREE BONUS: The Smashed Chef's Unique and Intuitive Wine Pairing Guide, Filled with Gourmet Tips & Tricks. *www.lovesharecook.com/smashed-chef.*

129

VODKA INFUSED FISH FAJITAS

COOK TIME: 16 MINUTES

Ah, vodka. The drink of choice for Russians and college kids. Bonus points if you go for a vodka-Red Bull: the modern frat house standard beverage.

Everyone loves a stereotype though, right? It was while cooking for a Russian client (whose name I still don't feel comfortable spelling) that I started seriously experimenting with vodka-based recipes.

Despite my misgivings, I actually found a lot of great uses for potato alcohol. For instance, this fajita recipe may now be one of my favorites. I'd still prefer to work with practically any other type of alcohol, but I'll admit vodka might have some uses. Happy now?

Ingredients

1½ pounds Mahi Mahi fillets, skin removed, cut into serving size strips
Sea salt and freshly ground black pepper
1 fresh lime
½ cup vodka
1 tablespoon olive oil
8 (8-inch) flour tortillas
Salsa Verde, recipe follows.
1 avocado, sliced

Preparation

- Get the grill going on medium high. Slice the cutlets of fish into one-inch strips; salt and pepper them, and sprinkle the fish with lime juice. Soak the fish in vodka for five minutes to get them drunk.
- Grease the grill with olive oil and cook each piece three minutes a side. Warm the tortillas on the cooler side of grill and then put them on a plate. Cover with a towel to keep warm.
- Assemble fajitas by putting fish, Salsa Verde and avocado on tortilla and folding them over after squeezing some tangy lime juice on top.

Salsa Verde:

1 ½ pound tomatillos
1 tablespoon fresh lime juice
½ cup finely chopped white onion
½ cup cilantro leaves
2 jalapeno peppers, stemmed, seeded and chopped
¼ teaspoon sugar
Salt and freshly ground black pepper

- Take the husks off of your tomatillos and rinse them. Cut each in half. Place cut side down on a cooking sheet lined with foil. Broil them for up to 7 minutes. Then take the tomatillos and the rest of the ingredients and put in food processor. Process in short bursts until you get a chunky salsa. Season the salsa to taste with salt and pepper. Keep in refrigerator. This salsa is also great for a snack with blue corn chips.

FREE BONUS: The Smashed Chef's Unique and Intuitive Wine Pairing Guide, Filled with Gourmet Tips & Tricks. *www.lovesharecook.com/smashed-chef.*

131

FAST GRILLED SALMON

COOK TIME: 23 MINUTES

Five in the morning, and I'm sitting on a boat clutching a bottle of whiskey. I don't know any sea shanties, but you wouldn't know it by the way I'm singing. "Singing." It's mostly nonsensical words, with a lot of humming in between. I am Captain Ahab. I *am* Hemingway's old man and the sea. I am one mind, in harmony with this beautiful vessel that carries me across the world's seven seas.

One of my fishing rods twitches. I pounce on it, desperately trying to reel in the catch of a lifetime. No matter how hard I try, the line just slips through my fingers. I take another swig from the bottle, calling upon it to give me some last-minute strength.

My client Tim found me a few hours later, sleeping on the deck of his boat with the fishing rod hooked to my jeans. That's right: the catch of a lifetime was no white whale, nor even a simple salmon. It was, in fact, *my own damn pants*. Thus—with a horrible sunburn, ripped jeans, and a dreadful hangover—ended my obsession with fishing.

There was enough fish stored up, however, to create this one last recipe. It's packed with nutrition, it's easy to prepare, and it's got plenty of spicy flavor. Just leave the fishing to the professionals.

Ingredients

½ cup extra virgin olive oil
¼ cup red wine vinegar
¼ cup red wine
½ cup pitted Niçoise olives
¼ teaspoon Chile De Arbol powder or cayenne pepper
2 cloves garlic, chopped
1 tablespoon Dijon mustard
1 tablespoon honey
Kosher salt and freshly ground black pepper
4 6-ounce salmon fillets

Preparation

- Blend the vinegar, wine, olive oil, Chile De Arbol powder, olives, mustard, garlic and honey together in a blender for a few pulses until you have a vinaigrette consistency.
- Put the salmon fillets in a baking dish and marinate with half of the blended items for fifteen minutes.
- Grill the salmon until well cooked on grill or using a griddle pan on medium high heat. It should take about 4 minutes per side. Season the fillets with salt and pepper to taste.
- While grilling, brush the remaining vinaigrette over pieces every minute or so. Serve when cooked through. I serve with white rice and sautéed veggies for the ultimate recovery meal. You'll need it, after your own drunken sailor story.

Smashed Chef Secrets: *When buying salmon you want to look for a nice, bright pink color. The flesh should be firm to the touch. When you press your finger into it, the flesh should bounce back. The smell should be fresh, slightly reminiscent of the sea and it shouldn't have a fishy smell to it.*

FREE BONUS: The Smashed Chef's Unique and Intuitive Wine Pairing Guide, Filled with Gourmet Tips & Tricks. *www.lovesharecook.com/smashed-chef.*

133

SMASHED SANTA FE TURKEY BURGER

COOK TIME: 25 MINUTES

I didn't grow up in America, though my parents hailed from there. Instead, I lived all around the world as a kid, exposed to all sorts of cultures and foods. Once a week, however, my mom would make the family food from the good ol' US of A to remind everyone of home.

A family favorite was burgers, though my mom was good about experimenting with new recipes. If she hadn't, I never would have found out that turkeys were assholes.

There we were, driving through Spain, when suddenly my mother let out a yelp. "What the..." A turkey, standing right in the middle of the road and glaring at us. Then it—understand, I have no better way to describe this—*flexed* its wings at us, walked up to our car, and started pecking at our bumper.

Now try to picture what you would do if a huge turkey came up and tried to fight your car. It was traumatizing to my young brain. I hope someone caught that turkey and did it justice. This single event is why I have no sympathy for vegetarians. I'm sorry, but some animals are just asking to be eaten.

Turkey burgers have never tasted as good as they did that night. Top this Southwestern-style burger with bacon just to be a real carnivorous jerk and assert your human dominance over every species.

Ingredients

8 slices applewood smoked bacon
1⅓ pounds ground turkey breast
¼ cup red wine
2 cloves garlic, finely chopped
1 large shallot or ¼ red onion, finely chopped
2 tablespoons chopped fresh thyme leaves or 1 teaspoon dried thyme leaves
2 tablespoons chopped fresh cilantro leaves, optional - parsley may be substituted
½ small green, yellow, or red bell, seeded and finely chopped
1 Serrano or jalapeno pepper, seeded and finely chopped

134

2 teaspoons, ⅔ palm full, ground cumin
1 to 2 teaspoons cayenne hot sauce, several drops
2 teaspoons grill seasoning blend (such as Montreal Steak Seasoning)
Extra virgin olive oil, for drizzling
½ pound deli sliced pepper jack cheese
4 crusty Kaiser rolls, split
1 cup sweet red pepper relish
Red leaf lettuce

Preparation

I prefer a nice white wine like a Chardonnay with turkey and this burger is no exception. Pour a glass and cook with me.

- Mince the garlic and chop the vegetables.
- Cook the bacon until crisp in nonstick skillet. Remove bacon, drain on paper towels and wipe out skillet.
- Mix the turkey, shallots, thyme, garlic, parsley or cilantro, Serrano pepper, bell pepper, hot pepper sauce, red wine, cumin, grill seasonings and salt/pepper if desired. Make four separate patties and drizzle them lightly with olive oil. Cook on medium to high in a 12-inch heavy skillet until cooked through.
- Put a slice of cheese on each patty and cook another 1-2 minutes. Put burgers on buns and top with sweet relish, red lettuce leaf and bacon. Serve alongside tortillas and an American flag.

STONE SOBER TURKEY PANINI

COOK TIME: 50 MINUTES

Sometimes, even the Smashed Chef has to take a break. For years now, I've dedicated the day after Thanksgiving as an alcohol-free day. A day to reenact ye olden days of American Prohibition, if you will. No wine, no beer, no whiskey, no *anything*. Stone cold sober, for one whole day.

Why? If you're anything like me, you shouldn't even need to ask that question. Thanksgiving, above all, is a celebration of glorious excess. Too much alcohol (in numerous forms), too much turkey, too much football, too much family time. That alone should be a good reason to dedicate the following day to Puritanical austerity. Well, that and the raging hangover I normally develop after Thanksgiving.

Okay, okay. It's mostly the hangover. The human body is not meant to drink wine, beer, whiskey, and liqueur in the same day, I tell you! Just take one day and let your body recover. Celebrate a *real* Thanksgiving. Give thanks that your extended family left and went home. Give thanks that you don't have to go shopping on Black Friday. Give thanks that you don't have to pretend to know anything about football (or even care) for another entire year. Give thanks that you can throw out your grandma's gross candied yams. Give thanks that you're not full of the heaviest food imaginable today, so you might actually get around to some recreational activities with your lover.

That's right. Suck it, Thanksgiving. We only tolerate you because it's an excuse to get drunk, gossip about our extended family, and eat turkey and stuffing. Turkey that you now, most likely, have far too much of in your fridge. Go ahead, make yourself a turkey panini (if you don't have a panini maker, just use a George Foreman grill like a pro), and relax all day. You deserve it.

Ingredients

4 Ciabatta rolls, split
6 ounces thinly sliced Fontina cheese
8 ounces thick-sliced turkey
½ cup cranberry relish
1 cup arugula leaves
Extra virgin olive oil

Preparation

Brace yourself. I know this is shocking, but like I said, this dish is stone cold sober.

- Start with one split ciabatta roll set side by side. Put about ¾ ounce of cheese on one piece of bread and put on a couple of ounces of sliced turkey.

- Add relish and about 5-6 arugula leaves to the pile and finish off with another ¾ ounces of cheese. Put the top slice of bread on and brush each side with olive oil.

- Using a Panini press, cook the sandwich until the bread is a nice golden brown. It takes about five minutes to finish a sandwich. Keep warm in the oven while making the other three sandwiches.

- Serve and thank me for helping you escape the excess of Thanksgiving.

CALIFORNIA CITRUS CORNISH GAME HENS

COOK TIME: 50 MINUTES

When's the last time you went out on a date that consisted of dinner and a movie? Or when's the last time you ate out, for that matter?

Must be nice.

Me? I'm banned from going on dates to restaurants, and most of my friends have enacted the same ban. It's quite simply, really. Inevitably I end up talking shop and utterly destroying everyone's mood. A typical restaurant excursion:

Friend: "This place is pretty good. I'm really digging this pasta I got."

Smashed Chef: "I guess this food would be good, if you *tripped and accidentally cut off your taste buds*. Blasphemer."

Cue friends staring at me, aghast. Cue date leaving in a huff. Cue chef of said restaurant crying. Not really, but close enough. It's just not worth it. Especially if I'm inebriated.

So yeah, instead I have to make my own food. Added benefit: I get to be the center of attention and hear people praise my cooking. Praise might as well be compared to morphine, for how addictive it is.

This dish was whipped up before one such "date night" which was actually spent not going out on a date. I hosted a double-date of sorts at my house, and I needed something that would spend more time in the oven than on the prep table. Enter this Southern California-inspired dish. It will taste just like you're in Orange County, except more like Orange County back when it consisted mostly of orange groves instead of asphalt.

Ingredients

6 hens, rinsed and pat dry
Coarse salt
Coarse black pepper
1 cup defrosted orange juice concentrate
½ cup white wine
1 cup aged balsamic vinegar
3 to 4 tablespoons extra virgin olive oil
7 to 8 stems rosemary, chopped

Preparation

Impress your friends by having them join you in the kitchen while you get dinner started. Let the wine flow and enjoy the laughter. Tonight, you will best your friends by showing what you can create with 5 minutes of prep time. "It's not a competition," you say? Wrong. It's always a competition, where cooking is concerned.

- Set the oven to 425 F. Take out 2 cookie sheets and line with foil. Cut the hens in half along the breast bone and put skin side up, six halves to a sheet. Use salt and pepper to season the hens.
- Mix the rest of the ingredients except for the rosemary in a small bowl with a whisk and pour over the top of the hens.
- Then sprinkle on the rosemary and allow to roast at 425° F for 15 minutes to seal in the juices.
- Have another glass of wine with your friends.
- Then turn down the oven to 375° F for another 30 minutes. Let rest for 5 minutes.
- Plate up the hens, 2 halves to a plate. Serve with grilled asparagus and crusty bread. Make fun of your friends' inferior cooking skills.

LAMB WITH SHERRY DRESSING

COOK TIME: 23 MINUTES

I can be kind of an ass sometimes. I freely and fully admit it. I've gotten better as I've aged, but still I amaze myself sometimes.

Even so, there's an ethical line I can't cross. I know, I can't believe it either. I've reached that line a couple times, in fact. I've even thrown rocks over that line, like some West German kid throwing rocks over the Berlin Wall. To no avail—I still can't cross it.

Maybe you're a worse person than me, though. Maybe you don't have a line. Maybe you're a sociopath. Feel free to try this one then. This one's free. It's something I debated doing to my niece and nephew as kids, but never could.

You see, my niece and nephew used to love this stuffed animal lamb they called Dolly. I toyed and toyed with the idea of hiding Dolly and making this lamb recipe, but I never could convince myself. Normally I was too drunk to act on my plan, and then was repulsed by it when I sobered up.

But good luck, readers who don't mind scarring children for life.

Ingredients

1 medium fennel bulb, quartered, core trimmed
2 cloves garlic
1 teaspoon kosher salt
2 tablespoons extra virgin olive oil
2 teaspoons minced fresh marjoram
1 pound butterflied leg lamb, fat trimmed
Freshly ground black pepper to taste
2 ripe plums, (recommended: Santa Rosa)
1 large ripe peach
8 cups mesclun salad greens (like mixed baby greens, in pre-packaged salad aisle)
Sherry Dressing (Below)

Preparation

A fruit forward wine like a Merlot or Cabernet pairs very well with lamb. Get drinking.

- Place the top rack of the oven six inches from the broiler and turn broiler on. Thinly slice fennel and soak in cold water.
- Smash or mince garlic cloves and sprinkle with a teaspoon of salt. Make the garlic into a paste with the flat side of a knife. Put marjoram together with olive oil and garlic and massage the paste into the lamb. Season with extra pepper.
- Put the lamb on a broiler pan and broil five minutes until browned. Turn it over and cook until internal temp of meat is 120 degrees.
- Rest meat for 5 minutes and put together peaches and plums, cut up. Put fruit in salad bowl with salad greens, adding the drained and dried fennel to the salad. Slice lamb into pieces and add to salad. Top with sherry dressing below and serve.

Sherry Dressing

2 tablespoons white wine vinegar
2 tablespoons sherry
2 teaspoons whole-grain mustard
1 teaspoon kosher salt
Freshly ground black pepper
1/4 cup extra virgin olive oil

- Using a whisk, combine mustard, wine, vinegar, salt and pepper. Next, whisk in the oil to make a thick dressing.

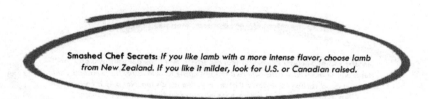

Smashed Chef Secrets: *If you like lamb with a more intense flavor, choose lamb from New Zealand. If you like it milder, look for U.S. or Canadian raised.*

FREE BONUS: The Smashed Chef's Unique and Intuitive Wine Pairing Guide, Filled with Gourmet Tips & Tricks. *www.lovesharecook.com/smashed-chef.*

141

SINGAPORE STEAK AND SCALLOP SURF 'N TURF

COOK TIME: 40 MINUTES

This is the tale of my best wingman accomplishment. I was in a Palm Springs loft, my client a wealthy, older celebrity gentleman. Earlier in the week he'd confessed to me that he was going after a much younger (like, really young) socialite. He just needed one good night to seal the deal. He needed something that could give him the stamina to go at it all night long, instead of crapping out halfway through. He said he wanted to "dance," if I knew what he meant.

I knew what he meant.

He turned to Asian cuisine. "Can you make something with lots of ginger?" he asked.

Ah, ginger, known as much for its aphrodisiac properties as it is for its flavor. I adapted a recipe I learned in Singapore, adding a surf and turf element for extra protein and endurance.

You'll have to take him at his word when he says it worked miracles. I didn't bother to check up on them after I served their meal. The noises kept me away.

Smashed Chef Secrets: Remember that old saying that "You get what you pay for?" This is one of those rare cases where it doesn't apply to cookware. The Smashed Chef prefers a good carbon steel wok. All of my chef friends do too. Not only is carbon steel less expensive, it also conducts heat more evenly for better stir fry results.

Ingredients

1 pound filet mignon steak, cut into 1-inch squares by ½-inch thick
1 pound medium size scallops, sliced in half
½ cup dry red wine, Syrah
1½ tablespoons minced ginger
¼ cup chopped scallions plus 1 tablespoon, for garnish
1 tablespoon minced garlic
3 tablespoons cornstarch
Peanut oil, to cook
3 tablespoons oyster sauce
1 teaspoon sugar
1 pound sugar snaps, both ends removed, blanched and shocked
1 cup chicken stock
Salt and black pepper, to taste
10 crispy rice cakes, pre-packaged

Preparation

- Marinate both the beef and scallops in red wine laced with ginger, garlic, scallions and 2 tablespoons cornstarch for 10 minutes.

- Using a very hot wok, add marinade and meats together, stir frying for just 2 minutes.

- Add 2 tablespoons oyster sauce plus sugar. Adjust seasonings and add snap peas only until they are heated completely. Make a glaze with a tablespoon of oyster sauce and chicken stock.

- Make a mixture of a tablespoon of stock and cornstarch and add this back in order to thicken glaze. Serve surf n turf with glaze over the top of crispy rice cakes.

- Add your favorite wine, and you may just get lucky tonight...

FREE BONUS: The Smashed Chef's Unique and Intuitive Wine Pairing Guide, Filled with Gourmet Tips & Tricks. *www.lovesharecook.com/smashed-chef.*

143

ROCK STAR SLOPPY JOES

COOK TIME: 25 MINUTES

One thing I've learned by working with rock stars: there's nothing better than a childhood favorite. All those things you thought were great as a kid? I hate to break it to you, but most of them suck now. Go re-watch your favorite childhood film. Or, actually, *don't*. Unless you were a precocious film buff of a child, it's almost guaranteed that you'll be disappointed.

If you manage to find a piece of your childhood that's still good after decades of neglect, however, you're in for a real treat.

One of my clients, "Steve," was a lead guitarist for a famous classic rock band (so famous, you probably had their poster on your wall at one point) and was always chasing that bit of nostalgia. Every once in a while Steve needed something to save him from drowning in excess, and I was there to help with his very own childhood favorite: Sloppy Joes. It became a pretty standard late-night meal for him.

Of course, this was a Smashed Chef twist on the traditional Sloppy Joe. I used a crustier roll to give it more of a gourmet feel, and added a splash of red wine for a richer, more complex flavor. Don't let the fact that it's a childhood favorite prevent you from drinking a fancy beer with your meal. It certainly didn't stop Steve.

Ingredients

1 tablespoon extra virgin olive oil
1¼ pounds ground sirloin
¼ cup brown sugar
2 teaspoons to 1 tablespoon steak seasoning blend, such as Montreal Steak Seasoning
1 medium onion, chopped
1 small red bell pepper, chopped
1 tablespoon red wine
1 tablespoon vinegar
1 tablespoon Worcestershire sauce
2 cups tomato sauce
2 tablespoons tomato paste
4 crusty rolls, split, toasted, and lightly buttered
Garnish: sliced ripe tomatoes, pickles

Preparation

Put a heavy 12-inch skillet on medium high and add oil. When shimmery, add meat. While the meat is cooking, mix brown sugar and Montreal seasoning. Put this into the skillet and add onions and red peppers. Cook on medium and add wine, vinegar, and Worcestershire sauce, cooking for about five minutes allowing liquid to reduce.

Finally put in tomato sauce and tomato paste and cook for five minutes more. Serve on fresh crusty rolls. Connect to your inner rock star.

PARMESAN GIN CHICKEN AND POTATOES

COOK TIME: 27 MINUTES

I was in culinary school (the first time around, not the second, successful time) when I first met Reuben, the alcoholic dog.

I always felt bad for Reuben. He was just one of a hundred other casualties emerging from the partying, culinary school life. He joined such esteemed ranks as my friend's totaled car, that one spot in my apartment where someone punched through the wall, and my really cool shoes that some girl threw up on.

Here's how it happened: fifty people would show up for a party, drinks would be spilled all over the ground, and Reuben would go around cleaning said drinks up with his tongue. If you've never seen a dog drunk, a) you're a much better person than I am and have lived a very noble life, but b) you haven't really lived. Of course, Reuben also loved snuggling up to girl's chests afterward, which made us even more jealous.

That dog was blessed.

Anyway, Reuben seemed to be partial to gin. Therefore, I'd like to dedicate the following dish to Reuben, the heroic, partying dog. He was truly an example for us all to aspire to.

Ingredients

1 ½ to 2 pounds red skin baby potatoes
1 small red bell pepper, seeded and cut into thin strips
1 Italian mild green pepper, seeded and thinly sliced
1 medium yellow skinned onion, thinly sliced
4 large cloves garlic, cracked away from skin
1 teaspoon crushed red pepper flakes
¼ cup tablespoons extra virgin olive oil, divided
Coarse salt and pepper
2 cups shredded Parmesan, available in tubs near deli -- make sure to get shredded cheese, not grated
4 (6- to 8-ounce) boneless, skinless chicken breasts, pounded flat
½ cup gin
4 plum Roma tomatoes or small, vine ripe tomatoes, seeded and chopped
15 to 20 leaves fresh basil, pile leaves, roll then thinly slice – chiffonade

Preparation

- Set oven to 500 F. Cut potatoes into quarters or halves. Cover a baking sheet with foil and put potatoes on along with peppers, garlic, onions and crushed red pepper flakes. Coat these with olive oil, salt and pepper. Cook in oven for 20 minutes. Toss the mixture halfway through. Put potatoes in serving dish.

- While potatoes are cooking, heat a large skillet on medium high. Put shredded cheese on a waxed paper cooking surface.

- Marinate chicken breasts in gin for ten minutes and then season the breasts with pepper. Place the breasts on top of the cheese and press down lightly to coat, repeat this on both sides of each breast.. When the oil is hot, cook the coated breasts for 7 minutes per side until cheese creates a crisp crust.

- In the meantime, mix chopped tomatoes and basil, adding salt and pepper to taste. When chicken is cooked, top it with tomatoes and serve alongside potatoes, onions and peppers.

- Pour one out for Reuben, while you're at it.

CHAMPAGNE ROASTED CHICKEN

COOK TIME: 30 MINUTES

I love Champagne for the same reason I love martinis (see my soup book for more information). You see, society has made Champagne a "celebration" drink. Every time you pop that cork, it's time to celebrate *something*.

Because of this aspect, which is pretty unique to Champagne, it's much more socially acceptable to drink way too much. After all, we're supposed to be happy! People who would blanch at drinking themselves drunk on whiskey have no qualms about drinking a comparable amount of Champagne. It's bubbly! It's fun!

Personally, I drink Champagne to celebrate getting drunk. You should try it sometime. Perhaps tonight, when you make this dish. Buy two bottles. Enjoy.

Ingredients

2½ pounds boneless, skinless chicken breasts, cut into large chunks
6 cloves garlic, crushed
3 tablespoons fresh rosemary leaves stripped from stems
3 tablespoons extra virgin olive oil
1 lemon, zested and juiced
½ cup dry sparkling wine
1 tablespoon Celtic sea salt and black pepper

Preparation

Pour a glass of Champagne and "celebrate." You can even say you're celebrating the act of cooking. Who's going to stop you?

- Set your oven to 450 F. Get out a 9 x 13 pan and put rinsed and patted dry chicken chunks in it. Sprinkle with rosemary, garlic, olive oil, grill seasoning and lemon zest.
- Roast for twenty minutes before adding sparkling wine and lemon juice. Turn off oven. Place pan back into hot oven with oven (off, but still hot) for about five minutes. Serve with lovely pan juices poured over chicken breasts.

Hey, you still have champagne left. More time to celebrate.

Smashed Chef Secrets: *The wine grapes most commonly used in making sparkling wine are Chardonnay, Pinot Noir, or Pinot Meunier. The term "sparkling wine" denotes all wines that have bubbles, however not all sparkling wine can legally be called Champagne. Only the sparkling wine that is made in the Champagne region of France can be designated Champagne. Both are still delightful.*

FREE BONUS: The Smashed Chef's Unique and Intuitive Wine Pairing Guide, Filled with Gourmet Tips & Tricks. *www.lovesharecook.com/smashed-chef.*

149

HANGOVER STEAK WITH MALBEC REDUCTION

COOK TIME: 40 MINUTES

Like many of these meals, I first made this steak recipe as a "cure" for an ailing client. This one was a high-profile marketing exec in California who could never say "No" for an answer when he was invited out to a party. As he said, "Marketing doesn't stop at five."

Have you seen the TV show *Mad Men*? Good, now you understand what kind of guy I'm talking about. Minus the whole "dark past" angle of that show. This was just another trust fund kid like myself, except spoiled and arrogant instead of a drunken genius like yours truly. He was a womanizer, an alcoholic, but great at his job.

One night my client's interminable come-ons caught up to him, however, and his face met up with some guy's fist.

I took him back to his place, gave him one steak to hold to his bruised eye and cooked the other steak with this recipe. I'm not sure he remembered much how it tasted the next day, but hopefully you will.

Ingredients

3 tablespoons extra virgin olive oil, divided
12 ounces rustic cut mushrooms
Himalayan pink salt, freshly ground pepper
4 tablespoons (½ stick) unsalted butter, divided
1½-pound hanger steak, trimmed, pounded ½" thick
Coarsely cracked black pepper
3 garlic cloves, crushed
1 5" sprig rosemary
2 tablespoons chopped fresh tarragon
1 tablespoon cut Italian flat leaf parsley for garnish
1 cup Malbec wine
¾ cup low-salt chicken stock

Preparation

- In a heavy 12-inch skillet on medium-high heat, add 2 tablespoons of the olive oil. Add rustic cut mushrooms and sauté for about 6-7 minutes, until they turn golden. Salt and pepper to taste. Transfer to bowl.

- Rub steak with salt and pepper. Add 1 tablespoon of butter along with the remaining tablespoon of the olive oil. Put in the steak and crushed garlic and cook for 3 minutes. Turn steak. Cook for 3 more minutes. (This is about medium rare) Remove from skillet and allow to rest.

- Using a slotted spoon, remove garlic and rosemary from the skillet. Drain all but about 1 tablespoon of drippings. Pour in the wine and let reduce for about 3-4 minutes. Stir up the remnants on the bottom of the skillet.

- Strain this mixture and add it back to the skillet. Add the stock and bring it to a rolling boil. Reduce this mixture to about ½ cup (approximately 4-5 minutes). Turn off heat and add butter and whisk until melted. Add the mushrooms and tarragon. Season to taste with more salt and pepper.

- Cut the steak into strips about ¼-inch thick. Add to plate and spoon over wine and mushroom reduction. Garnish with flat leaf Italian parsley.

FREE BONUS: The Smashed Chef's Unique and Intuitive Wine Pairing Guide, Filled with Gourmet Tips & Tricks. *www.lovesharecook.com/smashed-chef.*

|5|

TIPSY COTTAGE PIE

COOK TIME: 40 MINUTES

OK, it's time for a history lesson. Cottage pie can be traced back to about 1791 in either Ireland or Great Britain (they still argue about it, what a surprise). The potato became a staple food crop for the working class, because it helped stretch out more expensive ingredients like meat.

In 1877, some "genius" decided to change the name. Since many people used mutton, he called it Shepherd's Pie. For the most part, that name has stuck into the modern era.

Well there's only room for one "genius" in this cookbook, and it's me. I cling to the past. Thus, I present Tipsy Cottage Pie. And to make the Irish feel better, I booze-infuse it with Guinness (although my Irish pal thinks I should use Jameson Irish Whiskey).

Shepherd's Pie Cottage pie can take a long time to make, but this quick version has the same flavor in less than half the time. Just make sure to buy plenty of alcohol to go with it.

Ingredients

2 pounds potatoes, such as russet, peeled and cubed
2 tablespoons sour cream or softened cream cheese
1 large egg yolk
½ cup cream
¼ cup Guinness Draught
Salt and freshly ground black pepper
1 tablespoon extra virgin olive oil
1¾ pounds ground beef or ground lamb
1 carrot, peeled and chopped
1 onion, chopped
2 tablespoons butter
2 tablespoons all-purpose flour
1 cup beef stock or broth
2 teaspoons Worcestershire
½ cup frozen peas
1 teaspoon paprika
2 tablespoons chopped fresh parsley leaves

Preparation

"Here's to cheating, stealing, fighting, and drinking.
If you cheat, may you cheat death.
If you steal, may you steal a woman's heart.
If you fight, may you fight for a brother.
And if you drink, may you drink with me"

That is my favorite Irish toast. Cheers.

- Take the potatoes and boil for 12 minutes in salty water. Drain and put in bowl.

- While you're boiling the potatoes, take a large skillet on medium high and cook meat in oil, seasoning it with pepper and salt. Cook until brown and take off extra fat. Add Guinness and simmer for 2 more minutes.

- In the bowl of cooked potatoes, mix the sour cream, egg yolk and cream. Add this mixture to potatoes and mash. (Yes, again this is the time to think of your nasty boss and smash them good. I told you cooking is fun.) Add in the carrots and onion and cook five more minutes.

- In a small skillet, combine butter and flour over medium heat for 2 minutes. Put in the broth and using a whisk, add the Worcestershire sauce. Allow to thicken for a minute and add to the meat and vegetables. Put the peas in last. Spoon the meat and veggie mixture in a casserole dish and cover with potatoes and paprika.

- Broil this about eight inches from the broiler until potatoes are browned. Garnish with parsley and serve.

FREE BONUS: The Smashed Chef's Unique and Intuitive Wine Pairing Guide, Filled with Gourmet Tips & Tricks. *www.lovesharecook.com/smashed-chef.*

153

SHAGGY MANE CHICKEN

COOK TIME: 30 MINUTES

If you're a chef or an aspiring chef (which I'll assume is true, since you're reading this book), there's something you need to try once in your life.

Now, I'm not advocating usage of illicit drugs. It just so happens that I may or may not have worked with people who *did* use such substances. Lots of substances. If you're a chef who is also a praise junkie—and face it, we all are—then I pray you get the opportunity to feed your food to someone on mushrooms some day.

There's a first time for everything, and mushrooms certainly has given me a lot of firsts. For instance:

- First time I heard someone legitimately moan because my food tasted so good to them.
- First time I saw someone stare at a plate of food for an hour without eating any of it.
- First time I saw someone cry because their food "turned into a face."

Highly, highly recommended. Except not really. Also recommended: this recipe, which uses entirely non-hallucinogenic mushrooms (three different varieties!).

Ingredients

Salt
2 tablespoons extra virgin olive oil
4 6-ounce boneless, skinless chicken breasts
Pepper
2 tablespoons butter
12 baby Portobello mushrooms, sliced
12 shiitake mushrooms, stems removed and sliced
12 young Shaggy Mane mushrooms, sliced
1/3 cup white wine
2 large cloves garlic, chopped
1 tablespoon thyme leaves, chopped
2 large shallots, thinly sliced
2 tablespoons all-purpose flour
1½ cups chicken stock
3 tablespoons heavy cream or half-and-half
¼ cup chopped flat-leaf parsley
3 cups cooked rice, hot

Preparation

- Take a non-stick skillet and put over medium high heat. Season chicken with salt and pepper. Add olive oil and cook chicken for 5 minutes per side. Take out chicken and keep warm.

- Add butter to skillet and brown mushrooms for 4 minutes. Salt and pepper the mushrooms. Add the thyme, shallots and garlic, cooking for two minutes.

- Add the flour to your skillet, cooking for two additional minutes. Add the wine, stock, vinegar and cream. Heat on high for two minutes until it makes a thick sauce, stirring frequently.

- Slice chicken and add with parsley to sauce. Let it heat up over a minute in the sauce. Serve over rice.

- Any mushrooms that are good sautéed can be substituted, so if you have a mushroom connection…this dish has many variances. Just don't use *that* kind of mushroom, if you know what I mean.

FREE BONUS: The Smashed Chef's Unique and Intuitive Wine Pairing Guide, Filled with Gourmet Tips & Tricks.. *www.lovesharecook.com/smashed-chef.*

155

CONFUSED ASIAN LETTUCE WRAPS

COOK TIME: 25 MINUTES

It was my friend "Mike" who introduced me to Sake. He swore up and down that I'd love it, and I did.

Up until breakfast the next morning. Here's a tip from a seasoned drinking professional: when you go to a diner for breakfast, and you're drunk off too much Sake, *don't* stumble into opposite gender's restroom just because "your" restroom is locked. Yeah, I've yet to live that one down.

Even so, Sake is a good pairing for this recipe, which I've prepared in honor of Mike, my "confused" Asian friend. You see, Mike represents practically every heritage of the Pacific Rim. Part-Chinese, part-Japanese, part-Korean, part-Vietnamese—the list goes on and on.

This dish does the same. Lettuce wraps, which most people think are Chinese, are actually Korean. To make things even more complicated, I've added Hoisin sauce to the recipe to give it a bit of authentic Chinese flavor, as well as shitake mushrooms from Japan. Oh, and kimchi (or kim chee, whichever spelling you'd prefer).

Just don't get so confused that you enter the lady's restroom. Unless you're a lady, of course.

Ingredients

2 cups, fresh shiitake mushrooms
1⅓ to 1½ pounds chicken tenders cut into small uniform pieces
½ cup sherry
2 tablespoons peanut oil
Coarse salt and coarse black pepper to taste
3 cloves garlic, chopped
1 tablespoon fresh ginger root, grated
1 orange, zested
½ red bell pepper, diced small
1 6-ounce can sliced water chestnuts, drained and chopped
3 scallions, chopped
3 tablespoons hoisin sauce, available in Asian foods aisle
½ large head iceberg lettuce, core removed, quartered
½ cup kim chee (garnish)
1 navel orange, cut into wedges for garnish

Preparation

Did you pick up some sake yet? I hope so. Be adventurous. That's what the Smashed Chef lifestyle thrives on. Drink up.

- Take stems out of mushrooms and clean caps. Slice up mushrooms and cut chicken into small chunks.

- Heat a wok or skillet on high and add oil Do go out and shop for that wok if you don't have one. You will enjoy it, I promise. Put in the chicken for a minute or so and then add your mushrooms. Add the sherry along with salt, pepper, garlic, and ginger. Cook for another minute or two.

- Put the orange zest and bell pepper, water chestnuts (chopped) and scallions into your wok. Stir fry an additional minute and then add the Hoisin sauce, mixing it in thoroughly. Put chicken mixture alongside chunks of lettuce and garnish with orange slices.

- Eat a little bit of chicken with lettuce as a wrap and add kim chee to taste as a garnish.

- Enjoy with rice and more sake, if you'd like.

FREE BONUS: The Smashed Chef's Unique and Intuitive Wine Pairing Guide, Filled with Gourmet Tips & Tricks. *www.lovesharecook.com/smashed-chef.*

157

RED WINE-BRAISED SHORT RIBS

COOK TIME: 3 HOURS

"Hey, hey, hey! Everyone shut up! The cops are outside!"

Ah, the death knell of every party. Luckily our host, "Nat," had a gift for sweet-talking cops. Any normal party would have broken up when the cops came, but Nat talked them into turning a blind eye. The party continued, and everyone got back to their debauchery.

Everyone, that is, except Nat. "I know it was those guys across the street," he said, when I asked what was wrong. Nat was referring to the five (or maybe six) guys who lived across the street from his house. They were our age, but they scared the piss out of us. We never invited them to parties because we were afraid they'd start messing with the guests, and it was clear they resented us for it. This was too much, though. Involving the police?

Nat clearly agreed. "They've gone too far, Smashed Chef." He looked me straight in the eyes. "If I don't make it back, tell Chelsea I love her." He stood up, downed a quarter of a bottle of whiskey, flicked open a knife, and marched out the door. I ran after him.

Now, I can't repeat what was said that night. Let's just say I never knew Nat had such creative profanity in him, nor that he was so talented at making threats. And his neighbors never bothered us again.

These ribs are as primal as Nat's rage. Crack open a beer, bury your face in this meal, and try to recapture a little bit of what makes life worth living. Bonus points if you wield a knife while you eat.

Ingredients

5 pounds bone-in beef short ribs, cut crosswise into 2" pieces
Kosher salt and freshly ground black pepper
3 tablespoons vegetable oil
3 medium onions, chopped
3 medium carrots, peeled, chopped
2 celery stalks, chopped
3 tablespoons all-purpose flour
1 tablespoon tomato paste
1 750-ml bottle dry red wine (preferably Cabernet Sauvignon)
10 sprigs flat-leaf parsley
8 sprigs thyme
4 sprigs oregano
2 sprigs rosemary
2 fresh or dried bay leaves
1 head of garlic, halved crosswise
4 cups low-salt beef stock

Preparation

- Warm your oven to 350°. Season your short ribs liberally with salt and pepper.

- Now heat a heavy Dutch Oven, over medium high heat. Brown the ribs on all sides in small batches (a sear is all you want). Transfer to a bowl or plate and pour off all but about 3 tablespoons of the drippings from your skillet.

- Now add your carrots, onion and celery to the skillet and stir until onions start to caramelize. Add the tomato paste and flour while quickly stirring about two minutes until incorporated. The mixture should be a deep red.

- Now add the wine and stir again. Place in the short ribs and any juices that have flowed out onto the Dutch oven. Bring this mixture to a boil, then lower heat to medium and reduce the wine by about ½. This should take approximately 20-25 minutes.

- Once the mixture is reduced, stir in your garlic and fresh herbs. Add the stock, bring to a quick boil, cover the pan and place it in your preheated oven.

- Braise the ribs and cooking liquid in the oven until rib meat starts to separate from the bone, about 2 ½ hours. Place the ribs on a serving platter.
- Now strain the sauce that's leftover in the pan. Skim off the fat that rises to the top and season to taste with salt and pepper.
- Plate it on a bed of smashed potatoes with a drizzle of the sauce and steamed asparagus on the side.

CORNISH HENS AU VIN

COOK TIME: 50 MINUTES

My first round of culinary school, I was much like any other twenty-something kid. I fancied myself cultured. I fancied myself worldly. I went through a short phase full of mistakes. I bought a beret, just because I could. I smoked cigars because I thought they were more adult. I also became, "Wine Guy."

I love a good martini or a glass of whiskey, but wine is the classic "cultured" drink. Glass of wine in hand? Works great. In my infinite wisdom, I did some basic math. However, I neglected to remember that I was in fact a culinary student and not a math whiz. I thought, "If a glass of wine is classy, surely a bottle of wine is better?"

We all mistakes. Just don't make mine. It took three months before a girl called me a "Wino." Only then did I realize I looked like a combination of a homeless man and Che Guevara. Flattering.

Eat something actually classy tonight. This variation of the traditional coq au vin takes half the time to cook, and provides a light, hearty flavor. Beret and cigar not included.

Ingredients

4 slices thick-cut bacon
½ cup unbleached all-purpose flour
Kosher salt and freshly cracked black pepper
4 Cornish hens, about 1 pound each, rinsed and patted dry
2 cups dry white wine
1 cup water
3 garlic cloves

FREE BONUS: The Smashed Chef's Unique and Intuitive Wine Pairing Guide, Filled with Gourmet Tips & Tricks. *www.lovesharecook.com/smashed-chef.*

161

Preparation

Crack open the bottle of white wine. A Chardonnay will do nicely. Pour a *glass* before cooking.

- Heat up a large Dutch oven on your stove using medium heat. Add the bacon and cook until crispy. Remove bacon to a paper towel-lined plate and keep the bacon fat in the pan.

- In a large bowl, add the flour and salt and pepper to taste. (Don't be shy!) Put the game hens in the seasoned flour and coat them thinly and evenly. Put the hens in your Dutch oven with the bacon fat and brown on all sides of the bird. Add the wine and allow the mixture to come to a boil. Scrape off the flavor-filled browned drippings from the bottom as you stir.

- Now add garlic and water and bring to a boil again. Reduce heat to low and let simmer for about 20 minutes until hens are cooked thoroughly.

- Using tongs, remove hens from the pot. Tent them with foil to keep warm.

- Keep the liquid simmering to reduce and thicken. Season to taste with salt and pepper.

- Now add the hens back in the Dutch oven and heat through with the thickened liquid for about 10 minutes.

- Then put the hens on a serving platter and add crispy, crumbled bacon on top. Serve the gravy alongside to spoon over the hens. I usually serve this dish with prepackaged polenta, sliced and sautéed over olive oil.

MEATLOAF with PANKO

COOK TIME: 75 MINUTES

Alright, listen up. I assume you've already read my rationalization for making a less complicated meatloaf earlier in this book (Sherry Baby Meatloaves). Now let's get serious. If there are no kids around, you've got no real excuse to eat that ketchup-glazed blasphemy of a meatloaf. This is sophisticated meatloaf.

Seriously, this is like the Mercedes of meatloaf, if you were some sort of crazy person who ate a Mercedes. This is the Super Bowl, except you don't get to charge millions of dollars for commercials. This will utterly redefine your idea of what meatloaf is. Yes, Meat Loaf is more than just some washed-up singer.

If you bring ketchup anywhere near this Sistine Chapel of Meatloaf, I will have to turn to drinking to cheer myself up. Okay, fine, do it if you must. I'll look the other way *this once*. Just know that you will be ruining *art*. I should lie and tell you I got this recipe from an ancient mystic in India or something so that you'd take my warnings more seriously, but I won't because I could never lie to you. After making it this far in the book, you're part of my Smashed Chef family.

You'll also notice there's no alcohol in this recipe. That's because this is the last recipe in here. Feel free to drink all the alcohol to celebrate, instead of adding it to your food. I recommend Champagne for this celebration.

PS: Not really. Go with beer or whiskey or something. Champagne with meatloaf is just weird.

FREE BONUS: The Smashed Chef's Unique and Intuitive Wine Pairing Guide, Filled with Gourmet Tips & Tricks. *www.lovesharecook.com/smashed-chef.*

Ingredients

2 pounds Hamburger

1 egg, beaten

1 tablespoon dehydrated onion, or ¼ cup fresh diced

1 cup Panko Bread Crumbs

1 teaspoon salt

1 teaspoon pepper

Preparation

- Beef is easily "cooked" by body heat, so I like to wear a set of latex gloves to mix. So put on your gloves and gently mix the hamburger with the rest of the ingredients. Do not overwork or your meatloaf will be dense and tough like a Mafioso goon who has had a too many Irish Coffees.

- Now get out a cookie sheet and line the bottom with parchment paper. Form your meat mixture by hand into an oblong loaf. If you want to "cheat", use a loaf pan and finish by hand to make it more rustic.

- Bake on the parchment lined cookie sheet for about 1 hour. The internal temperature of the loaf should be 160°. Let rest for 5 minutes before serving.

- I prefer this loaf "crunchy" on top. If you like a glaze, however, use the same ketchup glaze as the Baby Meatloaf recipe earlier in the book. I promise I'll only judge you a little bit.

The Smashed Chef has one Golden Rule about booze-infused cooking:

NEVER cook with booze you wouldn't DRINK!

Let me explain. The real reason booze-infused cooking works so well boils down to FLAVOR. Each specific type of alcoholic beverage imparts its own specific essence. That means the better the booze, the better the taste.

Cooking wine and sherry sold in the food aisles of supermarkets are not only lacking in the flavor department, they also come loaded with added salts and preservatives. I NEVER use them as they can ruin the flavor of many dishes.

Shop for your wine in the wine department and your liquor at the liquor store or grocery. You will pump up the flavor of your dishes by using quality booze.

Of course you can take this too far. You don't need to use the most expensive wines, champagnes, beers, or liquors. In fact, many times I use wine in BOXES (cue gasps)! It's true. Many chefs are wine snobs and would call me out on this. I say *stuff it snooty chefs*, come join the rest of us in the 21st century.

There ARE quality wines you can find in boxes. My favorites are the Black Box wines. These wines have won awards and praise by *Wine Enthusiast* magazine, and I love to use them for cooking because the packaging keeps them fresh a long time (not that they usually LAST long).

Overleaf, I'll give you a short guide for selecting common wine, beer and spirits used in booze-infused cooking. Substituting any booze from a category on the list will give you the result you are looking for.

FREE BONUS: The Smashed Chef's Unique and Intuitive Wine Pairing Guide, Filled with Gourmet Tips & Tricks. *www.lovesharecook.com/smashed-chef.*

Dry Reds

- Cabernet Sauvignon
- Merlot
- Pinot Noir
- Syrah Zinfandel
- Malbec

Dry Whites

- Chardonnay
- Sauvignon Blanc
- Muscadet
- Pinot Grigio/Pinot Gris
- Viognier
- Sherry
- Fino
- Manzanilla
- Amontillado
- Pale Cream
- Cream
- Medium/Golden

Lighter Colored Beer

- Lager
- Pilsner
- Golden/Blonde
- Hefeweizen

Darker Colored Beer

- Pale Ale
- Scottish Ale
- India Pale Ale
- Amber Ale
- Stout

Whiskey

- Bourbon
- Rye
- Tennessee
- Blended
- Irish

Gin

- Distilled Gin
- Dutch Gin
- London Dry Gin
- New Western Style Gin

Claim Your FREE Smashed Chef Wine Pairing Guide!

You work too hard. You should be getting a massage right now. But you may not get one... So to comfort you, The Smashed Chef will get you the next best thing to relax you and fill you with happy chemicals that will course through your wondrous body.

In the form of wine, of course!

If there's one thing the smashed Chef gets asked often, it is...

What wine goes best with _____? (Fill in the blank.)

That's why I've created the Smashed Chef Wine Pairing Guide!

Inside, you will see my irreverent "new rules" for choosing a smashing wine for almost any meal you serve. The perfect wine enhances meals and puts you on center stage with friends and family. And with my Wine Paring Guide, you will know more than any of them when the conversation turns to what wine goes with what dish.

How does that sound?

All you need to do to claim your guide is go to my secret page for book owners only.

You can find it at *www.lovesharecook.com/smashed-chef*

(Diabolical, no?)

Just sign up for my newsletter and it's yours instantly. That's right, INSTANTLY. Don't you wish you could get instant gratification like that everywhere?

In the newsletter, you'll get my tips, tricks, and tactics for having more fun in the kitchen. Plus, you'll get my rants and stories of adventures that will make you giggle like a schoolgirl. And, I may even write of sausage, chocolate, and other heavenly delights.

So... what are you waiting for? If you want more of The Smashed Chef, get on the Interwebz and claim your stuff. Hey, it's FREE. It's fun. And it may just help you get more lovin'.

FREE BONUS: The Smashed Chef's Unique and Intuitive Wine Pairing Guide, Filled with Gourmet Tips & Tricks. *www.lovesharecook.com/smashed-chef.*

Made in the USA
Middletown, DE
06 October 2020